HOW TO SURVIVE THE CULT MUTATION?

VOLUME 1

And ye shall know the truth
and the truth shall make you free.
John 8:32

BY

BERNARD TOCHOLKE

ISBN: 978-1-957837-59-8

Contents

DEDICATION

I dedicate this book to the numerous people, whose families were rippcd apart by this cult. My family was only one of so many that I knew which where destroyed by this evil group of people. When you first meet them and decide to join them, they are maybe the most loving people you will ever meet. They will do practically any thing you might have need of. However, if you were with them for a while and then decide to leave, you will soon discover that they are the most evil people you have ever encountered in your life.

That is at least what I experienced. I was one of them for several years and I have to admit that I even enjoyed the gatherings they had. Gradually the cult mutation began and more rules were announced each year until finally I realized that they were straying from the contents of the Bible, and making up their own doctrine with each passing year. I saw many families, couples, and children ripped from each other. I am a survivor of this movement and I want to tell you TRUE stories of what I experienced while I was with them, and especially right after when I was shunned and removed from their group. I desire that you will find this book a warning not to get entangled with them. But, I will just share the many stories, and then let you make your own decision concerning your relationship with them. Is that a fair agreement?

I heard that some "common citizen" people, not part of the cult, voiced their opinion that they thought my first book, came across to them that "I had an ax to grind". They thought my writing was filled with anger against the cult, and therefore wrote it in such a way to make them look worse than they really are. I will lose that type of person as my audience, before they even get to my first chapter, unless I show right away some real alarming proof that it has gone too far towards being a cult. So first I will explain the past and then I must expose what is at the present.

When I met them in the early 1990's, they were just a very conservative group. No suit requirement, no vest, and few man made rules. However, the mutation towards a cult started with each passing year. I started seeing the dangers and started resisting the false issues. That led to my separation or excommunication from them in 2002. Now twenty years later, in 2022, I happened to see a youtube video that shows how far they have gone to being an anti-Bible cult. If you don't want to read the book any further, please watch the video, and I am sure you will not be tempted to go join them. My life and family would be drastically different if I could have had the privilege and tremendous gift of watching that video before I joined. And I hope it horrifies you also, and therefore saves you from the terror of false doctrine. But if it draws you toward them, then this book has also been a success in allowing everyone to see the cult's entire belief system, instead of how I got beguiled into it ignorantly.

Here is the video that is taken live, from their own sermons, and put together as a montage for you to see the facts, which they will hide from you if you just visit their "church".

- Https://youtu.be/8SQ_1M2S6Yw
- https://youtu.be/HryRvkRAXxl

Watching those two videos made me sick. If your church has doctrines I don't agree with, but are not eternal destination threatened, I will not make a scene nor argue with you. However, if it is like these two videos, filled with blasphemous statements and displays of extortion, I am compelled to respond against this evil. I hope this book will help at least one person to see the truth.

CHAPTER ONE
TRUTH HATERS

*"And with all deceivableness of unrighteousness in them that
perish;
because they received not the love of the truth, that they might be
saved.
And for this cause God shall send them strong delusion,
that they should believe a lie:*
II Thes. 2:10-11

There is a reason why the cult would hate this book.
Suppose you committed a crime, and let us assume it was murder.
Let us further suppose that you thought nobody saw you and that
you got away with it. However, for instance, I saw you do it while
I was hiding in the shadows. Would you love it if I started writing
about it; how you did it, when it happened, where you buried the
body, and the weapon you used? You definitely would not, even
though everything was true! The same goes for this book. I cannot
blame the cult for not liking the TRUE stories which I will write
about because it will reveal the full spectrum of who they are. They
only want you to see the image they are trying to portray in public.
However, the negative things about them, they wish were kept
secret.

Now there also are legal warnings. If at any time I do not
tell the truth, make up a story, or exaggerate what really happened,
it then puts several people in danger. I would be the first one in
danger of a lawsuit concerning SLANDER. Slander is when the
story is a lie and not true. The book publishing company could be
sued for slander also, even though they had nothing to do with the
lie, and they simply had assumed the author had written only truth,
which was not the case. Further down the line, but much harder to
sue, is the book store that sold the book. However, if the stories are
accurate and true, there is nothing anyone can do. The people that

it is written about will try to discredit it by calling it trash or dismiss it in any other way.

Another peculiar twist in the Judicial realm is that suppose I wanted to place a picture of the pastor in this book. Did you know that I would have to get written permission from him and provide it to the publishing company for them to include it in the book? Did you also know that the same rule does NOT apply to the Internet? As long as it isn't pornography, you could, without anyone's permission, use any photograph which was taken in public and place it on a website. So if you want pictures, go to the websites. But writing anything, as long as it is true, does not require permission at all and is never in danger for a Slander lawsuit.

Therefore, my zeal is to tell my TRUE experiences as honestly as I can. I also fear a much greater punishment of eternal consequence if I write a lie than getting sued for slander, which would not be good. If at any time I want to tell a story that I did not live or witness personally, I will mention that it is a second-hand story that I heard directly from the person that lived it or witnessed it.

There is one other thing also. I will write a lot of TRUE stories, but I will also have mini- Bible studies throughout the book, which they will not like. I will try to reason with scripture how they are wrong in their belief system. It is not a surprise or mystery that they will hate this book. But the reason I am writing it is for everyone to get the chance that I didn't get, of knowing their dark secrets before getting sucked into their midst ignorantly.

I have children caught up in this controlling cult that hates the stories in this book because often it is written about them and the terror that they had to endure growing up in this cult. Now, as adults, some of them will defend the movement vehemently and declare that my writings are trash. I don't recall them ever accusing my work as lies because they know the stories are true but just detrimental for their motive to attract strangers to their congregation. It sorrows me to see them not only hate the truth of the true stories but worse when they cleave to the false doctrine lies, which I hope to expose in this book.

Now I could start writing where and how I grew up, when I got married, about my children, how I met the cult and how it all came about of why I am writing this book. But I am going to do something very unusual now. I wrote a book more than a decade ago (2009?) where I expounded on what I experienced. When I wrote it, the horrid trauma of losing my family was still very fresh, and it is true, I was still very angry at what happened! As you read it, you might get that feeling that my emotions were running wild when I wrote it. However, I decided I didn't want to repeat the same stories in my second book, and it would be best to include the first book, **TORN ASUNDER, IN THE JAWS OF A CULT**, at the end of this book. Therefore, I highly recommend you read the back part of this book first. Then come back here and simply get an update of what transpired since I wrote the first one.

Two things I want to mention now. The first is about telling the truth. When a person has actually experienced a situation and is elaborating the details truthfully, the fact is that the story never changes. This same fact is not true if someone is lying. They forget the details of what they declared was true earlier, and the story changes as time goes along. I will condense the stories or just reference the earlier details in this first part of this book which I am writing now. Those early experiences are already twenty years ago when my family was ripped apart by this evil religious group.

The second point I want to mention now is the reason why I wanted to give an update on what transpired since the first book. Even after I wrote the first book, I had occasional nightmares. The expression or statement; (of being capable of taking the "person" out of a certain "place or concept" but unable to take the "concept" out of the person) is fairly true in this situation. "You can take the person out of the cult, but it is nearly impossible to take the cult out of the person! I had to get the cult out of me, and after one of those nightmares, I decided to list the reasons why the cult was ungodly and wrong. That list is what this book is about.

After I listed the points, which are the following chapters, which is also my updated mission, I have NEVER had another nightmare since, nor did I ever question again if I made a mistake about whether I left "God's anointed Church." Once I had the list and focused on the details, I gained a strong desire to write this book which hopefully will get into the hands of the many lives that have been torn apart by this ungodly threshing machine, which calls itself the Church of God Restoration (COGR). There are hundreds of lives they have physically and spiritually destroyed, and I hope this book will bring healing to many of them. So please read the original back book first, and then come back here. The first book was more about healing myself by talking about my experiences. However, my main desire for this updated book is to possibly provide some comfort, insight, and healing to the many individuals of the families that were ripped apart.

If you watched the two videos mentioned earlier, you already have an advantage that I never had. I just hope you already watched about 19 minutes with the first one and 15 minutes for the second video. I write this minute explanation because I had forwarded the link to someone who thought it was over after one minute when the first still image of scripture came up. I needed to clarify to them the length of it and to watch it to the end.

CHAPTER TWO
REVILERS

"Know ye not that the unrighteous shall not inherit the kingdom of
God?
*Be not deceived:...,nor **revilers**,... shall inherit the kingdom of*
God."
1 Cor. 6:9-10
Revilers, [ri-vahy-ler] noun. Someone who speaks abusively or
contemptuously to or of another person or thing.

My back was against the wall in a small room inside the
church building. The pastor, Patrick O'Shea, was standing in front
of me, shouting his opinions very loudly! His finger was stabbing
at the space just six inches in front of my face. He screamed, "You
will not get the children. Shereen will get the children. You know it
is a woman's state. You will lose everything! You will be
destroyed! You will die a miserable death and will then go to hell!
Is that what you want? We could have had you arrested for taking
your children to Minnesota without telling your wife. Shereen
needs to leave you!" He continued to yell at me for maybe thirty
minutes, with his spit flying out of his mouth and landing on my
shirt. At the time, I didn't know the laws, but later I found out he
was not only a reviler but also a liar at how I could be arrested.
Ignorance is not bliss, and I was scared at the verbal abuse I was
getting from the one who was my pastor at the time. In the carnal
mind, I wish I could have reached up quickly, grabbed his finger,
and then with a swift twist, break it. But I was too scared. The
group has a lot of power when they can control everyone by fear. I
hope you have read the longer version of this story from my first
book included in the back.

During that time of torment, I didn't care much for Pat
O'Shea and actually disliked him. Years have gone by, and the
wounds have healed. If I saw him stranded beside the road today, I

would definitely help him out. At the time, he tormented me on a weekly basis and meant it for evil, but like Joseph, God meant it for good. I am thankful that God led me out of that false doctrine, even though it was extremely painful!

Throughout the years while I was with them, I witnessed several times when members were taken behind closed doors with one or more pastors. When the victim finally is allowed to come back among the rest of the congregation, the victim is usually red-eyed from crying and visibly emotionally distraught.

I received a phone call from a man whose family was ripped apart. Now I did not hear or witness this phone call he had between one of the cult leaders, but if at any time the cult wants to dispute this story, I would be glad to have a public appearance with cameras to capture the entire discourse, which I doubt would ever happen. Because of my experiences, I believe the victim is telling me the true story. One of their main pastors got in a verbal argument with him, whom I will simply call Pastor Steve. The victim told me that Pastor Steve got so worked up that for a long duration on the phone, the pastor was yelling accusations at him, nearly at the top of his lungs. And then he yelled several times the same sentence, "YOU NEED TO GET SAVED," repeated over and over again! Doesn't it fit the dictionary's definition of a Reviler? I also know this pastor, and I also had my phone conversations with him. This same pastor threatened me and barred me from attending both one of my son's and one of my daughter's weddings. But the details are for a different chapter.

I know this "Apostle" Steve, when he was much younger, maybe a late teenager or early twenties, as I remember. His mother was a special sweetheart. This is a colored family, if that makes a difference. It does not to me. My family was treated like royalty when we needed to stay with them. They were poor, but they gave us the best treatment! You have seen him in the videos.

There was a meeting down in either Indiana or Ohio, and I don't remember which state. Members of the church have to become hosts of any members that travel a great distance to attend their meeting. Well, my family was delegated to stay with the

Hargrave family. It still is a pleasant past memory staying there. She was a wonderful mother raising several boys. Three of the boys did some special song practicing in the morning before the Sunday church service. Those boys could sing, and this wonderful young man, Steve, was one of them! Besides his screwed-up spiritual belief, I still like that man whom I haven't seen in years. I will mention him again in a later chapter. I still love that man.

CHAPTER THREE
CHILD ABUSE

"But whoso shall offend one of these little ones which believe in me,
it were better for him that a millstone were hanged about his neck,
and that he were drowned into the depth of the sea.
Matt. 18:6

What did you think about the many stories of child abuse from my first book? I believe in discipline because the Bible encourages it, if not downright demanding it. However, all the extra man-made rules of how it should be done, I don't believe, is what God intended. Smacking little babies like Danny Layne had preached, which I heard, is evil in my mind. And when my wife beat my son with maybe three to five hundred strikes, with a wooden stick is child abuse. That horrid picture of what my son's bottom looked like two days later is still permanently engraved in my mind well over twenty years later. I believe I will remember it to the day I die.

Beating a small child with a thick wooden dowel across the back of their hand is barbaric, in my opinion. I witnessed that often done by the pastor's wife, Sue O'Shea because her two or three-year-old child was falling asleep in the church service. That is cruelty!

Now let us suppose a hypothetical situation. Suppose we could convict one of these pastors of a crime that needs punishment. What if we applied the same rules to them? Would they be able to bend over the chair or couch and, without moving away, receive the same number of swats as their age, with a cane or sawed-off golf club? After all, Danny preached that you need a bigger weapon for discipline as the child gets older and bigger.

But reader, please be comforted because Jesus promised that every person will be judged, with the same (octane or horsepower) judgment that they judged others. If they were extremely critical at casting forth judgment, God would judge them in the same manner. So maybe if they disciplined harshly, they will receive HARSH discipline themselves.

CHAPTER FOUR
SICKNESS

*"He that turneth away his ear from hearing the law,
even his prayer shall be abomination.*
Prov. 28:9

I was with those people for almost a decade. During that time, I heard a lot of sermons and Bible studies addressing Divine Healing. They did not believe in doctors or medicine. I was reproved at least once for going to a doctor and once for buying my son an inhaler for his asthma. However, in all the years I was with them, NOT EVEN ONCE did I see a miracle of Divine Healing in their midst. I witnessed and knew several people who died. If it was a severe sickness, the member would die unless they go to the doctor, which is forbidden. But then I take that back and clarify it better. If you are a regular member, it is forbidden to go to the doctor. However, if you are a preacher like apostle Susan Mutch was, then you can get a C-section.

But a strange thing happened since I left. The cult has changed its view on that and allows members to go to the doctors now, that is, <u>if it is life-threatening</u>. They do not want any more additional stories which are in their archives, of their Hall Of Shames! One of my daughters, this last year (2021), received a C-section, delivering a baby girl at one pound and twelve ounces! The mother and baby would have probably died when Danny Layne was alive and in power. But I want to address this issue again in a later chapter.

One of their leaders, <u>apostle?</u> Elizabeth is a lady now whom I have known since she was a child. She was the daughter of Pat O'Shea, and I still like her as a person. She is very bubbly, and it was comical to me to see her debate a completely wrong situation when she was a child! She argued with me about the Greyhound bus, which she thought had a camel on the side of it,

19

instead of the noted racing dog! It was funny how I couldn't convince her it was a Greyhound dog. I met her again, just a few years ago, when she already had a family of her own. I still "righteously" love that woman, who is not a child anymore. But she became a preacher, and I don't agree with her spiritual views. That saddens me.

She stated some ironic things. I heard this from several sources. Since I wrote this chapter, I came across these videos mentioned already (at the beginning of this book), which proves the truth of what she said, and I had to add this sentence. There was a man sick in their congregation about to die. Liz made the announcement, claiming that God told her that the man would be healed. She doubled down on her statement by claiming that even if the man died, God would raise him from the dead! The man died and is still dead! What happened? Did God lie to her? Did she lie? Was she a false prophet? She still is one of their main preachers (apostles), even though all the claims were false and didn't happen. Did Jesus and the True Apostles of the New Testament ever declare something, and it didn't happen? The Bible warned that false leaders would rise and deceive many. I grieve for my children that believe their false claims.

"But the prophet, which shall presume to speak a word in my name, which I have not commanded him to speak, or that shall speak in the name of other gods, even that prophet shall die." (Physically? Spiritually?) *"And if thou say in thine heart, How shall we know the word which the Lord hath not spoken? When a prophet speaketh in the name of the Lord, if the thing follow not, nor come to pass, that is the thing which the Lord hath not spoken, but the prophet hath spoken it presumptuously: thou shalt not be afraid of him."* Deuteronomy 18:20-22

I have to make a correction concerning my first book. Remember the story about Gerry, the man with a hernia the size of a volleyball? I do not like that I had incorrect information when I wrote about it in my first book. I will change the name that was part of the story, and I will call him Jeff, but remember that is not his real name. There was a man in the congregation that had a small hernia, and Jeff was told to just try helping that member push the hernia back inside. Jeff was good with his hands and successfully pushed it back.

Shortly thereafter, Gerry had an accident and fell off the scaffolding and landed on concrete. The story continues according as I wrote the first time. However, when Gerry was dying, with the volleyball still outside of him, Pat O'Shea thought of what Jeff had done earlier. Danny Layne was definitely part of that story too, and those two men together devised the plan to have Jeff push Gerry's hernia back in. Jeff objected to the thought of doing something so huge, but in order to stay in good standing with these high-ranking "apostles," he has to at least go see Gerry and his situation.

When Jeff arrived, he realized that Gerry was too far gone and already in the process of dying. He believed the poison was already in the hernia, and if he tried pushing it back in, it would probably kill Gerry. He talked with Danny Layne on the phone and told him his thought and why he didn't want to even attempt this ordeal. Danny Layne then stated (false prophet, prophesy) that he believed that God would not allow Gerry to die and moderately forced Jeff to try. Jeff is still living with the guilt and mental agony of what took place. He tried pushing it in, saw it was no use, gave up, and headed for home. Other members were there when Gerry died just a short time later. Did some of the other men in the room try some more? I don't know.

Danny Layne had the typical response of forcing others to do the dirty work and then being able to say that he had nothing to do with it. He might have been in California, and his alibi was sound. Could it be from all his knavery and shenanigans he did for so many years that there is a rumor? Supposedly as he was dying, he did a lot of screaming. Did he see the flames of hell before he took his last breath? Or was this just a rumor with no truth? I need to find out. He did break up a lot of marriages which was forbidden in the scriptures. He also had a lot of other beliefs, contrary to God's teachings. He was not a nice man if you could see behind the front that he portrayed on the surface.

(I have finished writing this book and sent copies to three

individuals for editing. One of the individuals is James DeGraffenreid, and he called me this morning. He wanted me to write at least another paragraph to clarify something, so I agreed.) He told me that using a different name is evasive, and it would add more credibility to this story if I used real names. He is the man whom I changed his name to Jeff. James was my assistant pastor in Kenosha when I was getting tormented by Pat O'Shame; oops, misspelled! It is supposed to be O'Shea.

There was a man that came to Kenosha for his long vacation. Jerry Gossard was a very kind man who lived on the East coast, and I think it was Maryland. He had an extremely well-paying job, a house, and property. His job gave him, I believe, three or four weeks of vacation each year. There was no cult congregation in Maryland, so for his vacation, he came to Kenosha. Our Pastor Rat O'Shame allowed him to preach several good messages, which were Bible-based. However, the weeks went by quickly, and his vacation was used up. He told me he needed to go back home until next year.

That is when this apostle Rat O'Shame became dictator over Jerry. He told him that a well-paying job is not worth more than his soul. He demanded that Jerry should stay in Kenosha and call his company, and without giving them any notice, just quit! His house could be sold without him being there. Absurd! But Jerry dared to defy this Rat god and left for his home anyway. I immediately noticed the removal of the prefix "Brother" in front of Jerry's name. He had preached just a few days ago, but now this Rat had unsaved him. Once unsaved, Jerry will never be a preacher again according to the cult's rules, and by what I witnessed. I am sure Danny Lame (Layne) had also called him and gave a tormenting speech to him.

Trying to redeem himself, Jerry gave his company a two-week notice and quit his job. He also sold his house, as far as I recall. He returned to Kenosha with the dictator's Rat thumb on his neck. No longer was he a preacher, but just a humbled misfit that violated O'Shame's demands. I was excommunicated just a short time after that, but I still remember that Jerry was kind to me, unlike the conduct of the apostle rat! James DeGraffenreid was my assistant pastor, and he also never showed any ungodly behavior towards me. Therefore, I wanted to hide his identity from the evil thing that happened after that. But James asked me to include his identity!

Jerry was, I think, in his fifties when I left. Anyway, he is the person that got the small hernia. James was working nights during that time. When James came home in the morning, he found out that Prideful Pat O'Shea had tried for several hours during that night to push the hernia back in but couldn't do it. So, he asked James to try. James was good with his hands and did it in a fairly short time. That is when the other Gerry, with a hernia the size of a volleyball, came into the scene.

Pastor Rat O'Shame, (oops, Pat O'Shea), called Danny Lame, (Damning Lame), (or is it Layne?), and the two men "forced" James to give it a try to push Gerry's hernia back in. James protested against it, stating that infection and gangrene were more than probable inside that "volleyball." Unless you have been a victim of this cult, you cannot comprehend the pressure they can put on their members. Nobody put a gun to the head of James, nor to the heads of the three hundred people that drank the poison Kool-aid in Jonestown. After James believed the false vision of the Chief pastor, Damning Lame, declaring that God wasn't going to let Gerry die, James attempted it without success. Gerry was still alive when James headed back to Kenosha. A thing for rejoicing is James left the Cult also, several years after I did. Jerry died years after this hernia situation.

CHAPTER FIVE
BIBLE REVAMPING

"If any man shall add unto these things,
God shall add unto him the plagues that are written in this book:
And if any man shall take away from the words of the book of this
prophecy,
God shall take away his part out of the book of life,.."
Rev. 22:18-19

This chapter will be a little longer since there are several Bible additions or alterations that they have done, which I believe are wrong. However, I will let you decide if they are wrong.

1. **Brother & Sister.** I believe I addressed this topic in the first book. It is blasphemous for them to think they have more light on the demanded prefix of using Brother or Sister each time they say the name of one of their members than Jesus did. Search the New Testament and find just ONE instance when Jesus said, "Brother Peter, or Brother or Sister (whoever)." It isn't there! That add-on is used for controlling the members. I prefer using the term as much as Jesus did.

   Some of us have left this Babylon, called Church Of God Restoration (COGR). However, out of habit, we still want to use a prefix (identical to the cult doctrine practices), apply this prefix "Brother," and add it onto the names of other individuals that also have left the cult. Individuals like myself feel nauseous by just remembering how the cult used that term to control their people. Jesus did not call him Brother Peter while he was still teaching, but then just called him Peter, after he denied Jesus three times! Then after he arose again, Jesus didn't address him again as Brother Peter. The term "Brother" was never used as a leverage tactic. I wish we could all outgrow the influence Babylon had on us, and follow the example of Christ. Sure, Jesus said that they were his Brethren. But he did not beat them up using a title.

2. **Their belief in "One True Church."** During the 1990s, they believed and preached that they were the ONLY One True Church, and everyone else was lost in Babylon. They might have salvation, but if they do not join their Church of God Restoration movement, they are not saved anymore if that person rejects joining them. Ironic: *"And the Lord added to the church daily such as should be saved." Acts 2:47.* What that means from a Berean's point of view is that God had established a church in the Book of Acts after Jesus was crucified, then continued building his Church another 2000 years, but now his "building" is worthless unless you join this cult! Today you might be saved, which automatically puts you in the Church that the Lord built. You are in the Church as long as you don't cross paths with the COGR because immediately then, you are no longer in the True Church. The cult is the Real Church, and the Lord's Church is the false Church or the Incomplete Church? Crazy philosophy!

   "I am the way, the truth, and the life, no man cometh unto the Father but by me." John. 14:6 Did Jesus tell a lie? Because if you go to Jesus but haven't joined the Cult yet, you still can't go to heaven according to them. Getting salvation is not good enough, but joining the Cult means everything, and they rejoice when someone joins them. So once again, Jesus alone is incomplete, and Jesus needs the Cult to secure his followers to heaven? Absurd! Ridiculous!

   If you have watched the first two videos, you will have seen how they bow down to their Chief apostle, Ray Tinsman, instead of Jesus Christ. They are told they are good members if they pray through that man! That's blasphemous!

3. *"After this I beheld, and, lo, a great multitude, which no*

man could number, of all nations, and kindreds, and
people, and tongues, stood before the throne, and before
the Lamb, clothed with white robes, and palms in their
hands." Rev. 7:9 If this cult is the One True Church, then
the second coming of Christ is a VERY long time in the
future. When Christ returns, it will be a number that no
man can count. The cult at best has maybe three thousand
members (just a guess). Can you count that high? I know a
lot of people can. But God said no man could count that
amount. There are also about 195 Countries in the world.
The cult has members in maybe a dozen or less of those
Countries. And what about different dialects within the
same Country? So IF the cult has it correct, that they are
the Right Church, then the Return of Christ is a long time
away, unless the Cult is wrong! What do you think?

4. *"What therefore God hath joined together, let not man*
    put sunder." Matt. 19:6 This topic alone should condemn
    the cult by itself. It is difficult to guess how many
    marriages they tore apart, but I think it is in the triple digits.
    "And the woman which hath an husband that believeth not,
    and if he be pleased to dwell with her, LET HER NOT
    LEAVE HIM." 1 Cor. 7:13 Both of these verses are
    commands. However, Danny Layne always used the story
    of Ananias & Sapphira. It was their land that they sold and
    were allowed to keep all the money they wanted to keep.
    However, the couple wanted the praise of men but yet
    wanted to keep some of their money secretly.

    So they devised a plan to agree together, to lie to the
    Apostles, that they sold it for a cheaper price, but keep the
    difference. They decided to come in at separate times and
    declare the same lie. The Apostle struck the first one dead
    for lying to the Holy Spirit, and when Sapphira came in a
    little bit later (about three hours), not knowing that her
    husband was dead, told the same agreed lie again to the
    Apostle and was rebuked and also dropped dead.

    Danny Layne used that scripture and took it out of

context. He said that she didn't need to die if she had left her husband. But because she stayed with him, she was also ordered to drop dead. Danny (the false prophet), which couple did you break up that you knew wanted to lie to the Holy Spirit? You did tear apart many couples just because either the husband or the wife didn't want to follow your false ways. Refusing to follow a false way does not represent lying against the Holy Spirit. However, Danny Layne has died, but the Cult leaders are still practicing tearing families apart just because one spouse is not deceived by their false doctrine. I believe Eternity will be unpleasant for those false teachers.

5. ***"Then the LORD said unto me, The prophets prophesy lies in my name: I sent them not, neither have I commanded them, neither spake unto them: they prophesy unto you a false vision and divination, and a thing of nought, and the deceit of their heart. Therefore thus saith the LORD concerning the prophets that prophesy in my name, and I sent them not, yet they say, Sword and famine shall not be in this land; By sword*** (word of God?) ***and famine*** (spiritually?) ***shall those prophets be consumed. And the people*** (followers) ***to whom they prophesy shall be cast out...: for I will pour their wickedness upon them."*** Jeremiah 14:14-15

Does this scripture qualify for the vision or prophesy apostle Elizabeth said, about the sick man, that he will be healed and possibly be even raised from the dead? Neither of those things happened, and the man is still dead. The flesh has already rotted away, so when will the bones jump out of the grave to validate that her prophecy was not a lie?

I already mentioned in my first book how Danny Layne usurped his own thoughts as gospel truth. He declared that pet names or nicknames are not saintly, or worse yet, ungodly. Isn't it a shame that he knew more Godliness (sarcasm) than Jesus Christ? Did not Jesus

27

violate Danny's command? Did not people warn Jesus that Herod was looking to kill him, and Jesus told them to go "tell that fox" (Herod) and say that his (Jesus's) time was not yet fulfilled? Did he not have a nickname for Peter, "The stone"? Who did he call "Sons of Thunder" or "whited sepulchers" (caskets)? There are many nicknames, even hostile names, that Jesus called others. Therefore, these cult members need to decide whether to believe Danny Layne or Jesus Christ.

Another person that I heard preach his opinion from the pulpit was "apostle" Pat O'Shea. He disapproved of me working nearly every Saturday to pay for the bills and again prepare financially for the next highly (guilt-trip) recommended a camp meeting. Therefore, he preached on Sunday that it is NOT right to work six days a week, especially when we have a family. He claimed five days was the Godly thing to do and spend Saturdays with our family. Once again, there is a problem because God gave us an example. God worked six days and then rested the seventh day. Does that mean that Pat O'Shea is smarter than God? The cult members need to also decide if Pat O'Shea is superior to God or if Pat is adding to the Holy Bible and is a false prophet. Repeat: It is dangerous to add to scripture.

I also remember him preaching that "the Bible said that we are to cut our throats if we are eating like a glutton." He was behind the pulpit moving his hand back and forth across his throat like he had an invisible knife. When I heard that, I was already in trouble with him and was already noticing a lot of false things about this, "One True Church." I knew what he was referring to, but incorrectly. *"And put a knife to thy throat, if thou be a man given to appetite."* Prov. 23:2. I wish I would have had the courage to challenge him by speaking up in the congregation, and ask him where that was at, and then having him read it. After reading it, I would offer to put a knife to my own throat while he cuts his throat to demonstrate if he was "adding to scripture." Which one of us would live longer, or would we both die together if I just put a knife to my throat to force me to extremely consider if I was becoming a glutton?

Cult members, are you following these apostles blindly who are in the practice of feeding you things that were added to the Holy Bible? The Bible states that not only the people that lie, but also, they that love the lie, will be in danger at the judgment. This cult is NOT so pure when you measure or compare them to what the Word says. They are more loyal to people that follow them than they are to the truth. Here is an example.

Around 2000, I remember three of their pastors chose to leave this cult. As soon as that happened, ALL of these ministers' past sermons became contraband. You not only could not buy them from their publishing place, but we also were ordered to throw away all the tapes we had of them. Now let us consider that situation. The cult agreed with what the pastors had preached before. But now, it was evil. Does that mean that the truth changed and what they said was no longer true? Remember Balaam in the Book of Numbers and the Donkey? Even the donkey was remembered for speaking the truth even though he was not a Christian. The rooster also that crowed when Peter denied Jesus three times was remembered for speaking the truth. He also was not a member of this assumed "One True Church" that this Cult claims they are part of, but his "speech" is still noted today. The truth will always be truth, and lies will always be lies. However, this cult adheres to people more than truth. If they dislike the person, the cult will condemn the truth they spoke. Remember the C-section their prominent female apostle had? They needed her, so they covered up their "sin" to keep her, which would have meant ex-communication to the common member. But the truth is that the donkey, the rooster, or anyone that

29

leaves their group, immediately becomes sin and contraband.

This book speaks truth against them, and if they had a desire for the truth, they would listen to it. However, they love their own agenda and their many fabricated beliefs and despise truth. Therefore, I am convinced that I did NOT leave the One True Church (that Christ built) when I left them. There would be hope for them if they had the Godly spirit of King David. 2 Samuel 16:5-13 He encountered the man, Shimei, that came toward him, cursing David and throwing stones at him. The cult is more like Abishai, that demanded that they should cut the man's head off. However, David recognized that there was partial truth from God in this man's cursing, accepted the truth, allowed Shimei to live, and kept cursing the truth sent from God.

6. **Doctrine of which parents to respect, or not.** There are numerous verses in the Bible about children needing to obey their parents, even when they are old. There is a balance, though; I understand that. But this group will take one particular verse out of context and ignore all the other scripture on the matter. They then "add to scripture" to explain what that one verse means. They use Ephesians 6:1 *"Children, obey your parents in the Lord: for this is right."* They focus on the words *"in the Lord"* and say that children do not need to obey anyone that is not with them because if they are not with them, they can NOT be *"in the Lord."* Children do not need to obey or respect a parent that has left this cult! I talk from experience where your children are rude, disrespectful, and right down evil in your face. When I bring up scripture about respecting or obeying their father, they hatefully spit out the verse above and say they do not need to be kind to me.

Could *"in the Lord"* be similar to the English word "AND"? I am referring to Cult techniques of interpreting scripture. Doesn't that word "And" mean "in addition" or "also"? So from a (sarcastic) Cult version of interpretation, were there not three people in the manger? Because, when the shepherds came, didn't they find, "Mary, and Joseph, **AND** the babe lying in the manger"? Three people, right? Out of sarcasm, this is your first lesson in Cult interpretation! Understand their techniques!

Back to "in the Lord" disrespect. There were times when I had nothing but grief picking them up for my court-ordered visitation. They destroyed things and often made a mess intentionally. One example was when they gathered all the loose paper they could find in my car as we were traveling to take them back home. Newspaper, maps, receipts, any document was placed in the floor indentation in the back seat. Then about a gallon of water was dumped on the paper to make a soggy mess. I didn't find that until after I had dropped them off. That was the behavior of children of the One True Church! Delightful, isn't it?

It was not them, actually, though, because I saw through it and saw where the evil fuel was coming from. The cult meant it for evil, but God used it for good to show me the group of who they are. I saw movies and actual instances where a child is screaming and hysterically crying when they are ripped out of the arms of one parent whom they loved and taken to the other parent or foster home. If my children had given me that kind of a display of love, wanting to be with me, instead of the hateful actions they did do, the separation after each visitation would have been unbearable compared to the torment they did give me.

I love the fable of the wind and sun competition. The wind boasts that it is stronger than the sun and arranges a challenge. The wind asks the sun if he sees the man way down there on the ground. He said, I believe I am stronger because I can blow that coat right off of him, which I doubt you can. So the sun agreed, and the wind started blowing. The more the wind blew, the stronger the man grabbed onto his coat and pushed against the wind. Exhausted, the wind gave the sun a chance. The wind was wicked, but now the sun showered the man with warmth and light, which represented love. Without a request from the sun, the man took his coat off by his own will. Hate is strong, but true love is stronger.

There was no desire for me to return to the cult when all I saw was hate. They meant it for evil, trying their best to blow me back to their lies. However, it was God's blessing for them to blow ungodliness and evil winds upon me. If they had loved me after I left them, or actually when I got pushed out, I probably would then still be there! That would be horrible, being deceived under their spell and false doctrine, and therefore in danger for eternity. I am glad God squeezed them, which caused the evil "toothpaste" which was inside of them to come out. That made it easy for me to know I didn't leave a "Christlike" or a "Godly" church. This cult is the most hate distributing people I have ever met in my life!

CHAPTER SIX
CLOTHING DOCTRINE

"...and be clothed with humility...."
1 Peter 5:5

One of the most obvious visible features of this cult is their clothing doctrine of how to dress. Most of their rules are made up by their leaders, with very little Bible backing of scripture that outlines exactly what to wear. They look like they are in the 1800s, but even back then, many of those clothes the cult would consider un-saintly. So where can we go IN THE BIBLE, to get a little idea of what we need to wear? Let us consider the chosen people of God throughout the Bible.

Throughout the Bible, there are a lot of examples of dress codes without preaching a doctrine on them. Joseph was sold into Egypt by his brothers. He was chosen by God, who also protected him. Much later, a famine broke out, which caused his brothers to come to Egypt to buy food. Why did not even his brothers recognize him? Did he not dress "Saintly" like this cult would have him dress? How could he be of God if he didn't dress like this cult teaches? From the perspective of all his other brothers, they saw a man that walked, talked, smelled, and dressed like an Egyptian, and according to what this cult teaches, it would be impossible for him to be chosen by God.

What about Esther? An evil man devised a plan to kill all the Jews and ordered the King to sign a law to allow that to happen. Esther was one of the King's wives, and the common people did not know that this Queen was a Jew. Even the King, her husband, did not know she was a Jew. Why would they not suspect that if the dress code which is fabricated by this cult was standard in Godly apparel? Were the people, rulers, and King visually blind? Contrary to the cult doctrine, the real truth is that Esther blended in with the common people of her day or dressed like the typical queen should, and yet chosen by God for a purpose.

The cult might object or argue that these are all Old Testament examples. Let us look at the New Testament to see if they dressed like the cult. The Roman soldiers, along with the Scribes and Pharisees, often tried to figure out who Jesus was. Judas offered to kiss Jesus so the soldiers would not need to identify him themselves and accidentally get the wrong person. The objection, maybe by the cult? It was because he was with the disciples, which all looked like this cult with their dress code. Really? Then why later, when Peter wanted to get close to the action to find out what was happening to Jesus, why could not the general public identify him that he was one of Jesus's disciples? If the cult members had been the disciples, and if the crucifixion was today, only a blind person could possibly not identify them by their dress. When Peter was accused, they did not say, "your clothes betray you," but it was his speech or dialect.

A few hundred years later, the Christians met a lot of persecution and death. They hid in the Catacombs, which were a maze of underground tunnels. However, they had to surface once in a while to get supplies and food. If they had dressed like this cult, they would have been exterminated immediately. It is commanded in scripture to dress modestly. Did this group add to scripture all their thoughts and opinions of what modesty is? Certainly! Carnal men are not supposed to lust after these cult women if they dress Godly. Could it not be possible that carnal men could lust after them anyway, because of their face and also their totally exposed neck? These women pile their hair on top of their heads, exposing their naked necks! For that cause, the women should dress like the Muslim women, with only their eyes exposed, which is a lot more modest than how the cult dresses. I added that out of sarcasm, permeated with a ton of truth. So, could modesty not be more of a custom or culture than a set of rules designed by Danny Layne and their leaders in charge? Lust will happen, regardless of what clothing the women wear, unless they are totally hidden with only their eyes being seen.

CHAPTER SEVEN
EXTORTIONERS

"Know ye not that the unrighteous shall not inherit the kingdom of
God?
*Be not deceived:...nor **extortioners** shall inherit the kingdom of*
God."
1 Cor. 6:9-10

Extort / (Extortioner) [ik-'stort]. To obtain by force or improper pressure;- cheat, swindle, coerce, compel, force, trickery

Do you remember reading in the back of this book how the cult cheated themselves into obtaining the church and pastor's house in Kenosha, Wisconsin? They were NOT upfront with the former members that we had a desire to be the main visible congregation now. Instead, we made it seem like we were only renting it for the weekend. A few former members came to our special meeting, but our members were told to NOT let the secret out that we would soon be the owners of this property. If they don't show up for our secret election of putting Pat O'Shea in charge, it will be the first step in this extortion scheme.

Move on to the second step after that. There were less than five former people still occasionally coming to every Sunday service. However, if we secretly notify only the cult members that we will have a secret voting night, the former members were cheated out of voting to the disposal of their building. The cult voted then to donate "their/ this property" over to the Church Of God Restoration Trust Fund, indirectly in their Minister's control. It was almost paid for by the former members. And for about twenty thousand dollars (which included repairs), **extorted** nearly a half a million-dollar property. It was nauseous to read in their next Cult's paper how richly God blessed them!

I heard another story that some of their members gained information on their boss's business whom they worked for. Once they had the information they needed, they quit that company and started their own company. It was in direct competition against the boss. They just quit. They had the detailed contract list and then went to all the customers of the ex-boss and coerced them into switching their business to themselves. I found out about that chicanery from someone that saw it happen approximately around the year 2000, I think.

Suppose one of their members decides to leave the cult. Suppose that the Cult's Chief Apostle knew who the ex-members boss was. The chief apostle will go to the former member's workplace and apply pressure on the boss until he fires the ex-member! I have seen that happen. Does that fit the definition of "improper pressure"? What a wonderful Godly Church Of God Restoration! Or do you not agree? I don't. But it is your thought that matters, not mine.

They are also a Master of Deception, but I don't want to try elaborating an entire chapter on how they deceive; Judges, police, any informant, and easily the common public. What they say, what you hear, what you understand, and what they secretly mean with all their intentionally double meanings are all part of their crafty ways. You need to ask the question in twenty different ways to try to get the answer that is closest to the truth. Don't believe the first response they gave you because they didn't really answer your question. Remember, they only gave you a misleading response, not an answer.

Now I will let you be the judge. You can only take this test if you have watched the two videos mentioned. Remember how their apostle went down to Mexico and preached the message that they better donate a LOT OF MONEY that very moment, or they would not be saved anymore. Look at that video again if you need to refresh your memory. Now you see the definition of "Extortion" as the heading for this chapter and compare that to the sermon that man preached. Do you think that sermon was extortion? And what is your idea from your answer? How does it relate to the Bible verse mentioned above that definition?

I will ask you to decide if it was extortion of what their

apostle Steve Hardgrave told me. He ordered for me to take my website down and claim that my book was all false before I would be allowed to attend either my son's or my daughter's wedding. Does that fit the definition of extortion? Improper pressure? Coerce? Compel? Force?

CHAPTER EIGHT
EVER-CHANGING SAND DUNES

"Jesus Christ, the same yesterday, today, and forever."
Hebrews 13:8

In the last thirty years, I have seen and heard of a lot of changes. I was not with them in the last twenty, but I am amazed at the constant change of doctrine. When I started with them back in the early 1990s, I received silent treatment for about a minute for telling a funny joke. That silence was deafening and a rebuke to me. Recently, I heard that ministers tell each other jokes.

The anti-Doctors and anti-medicine doctrines have also changed. I can't take a lot of credit, but I believe my first book and website had a little bit to do with that change. Members are allowed to go seek medical attention now if it is life-threatening. But I emphasize that it has to be life-threatening!

Many of the entertainment things were condemned back when Danny Layne was alive. Air shows were bad when I was with them. My ex-wife condemned me for wanting to take my children to OshKosh, the largest airshow, and pulled the fancy stunt of getting me arrested. However, this last year of 2021, she herself went to the place! Times change in their belief. A lot of the things I fought against back then are now acceptable. My ex moved several years ago down to Mexico but comes to the United States a few times a year. Ensenada, Mexico, down the Baja peninsula, south of San Diego, CA, is where she resides most of the time.

Before I forget, apostle Steve Hargrave, I understand, is the second most powerful in that cult. I received calls from him on two different occasions. Once when my son was getting married, I had a phone call with him. They hate my first book and my website. He told me in order to attend the wedding I would have to declare that everything I wrote was false!. I told him the book is only about true stories. He told me it was only from my perspective. Is the Bible wrong, too, because it is all made up from the disciple's perspective? Oh, he got angry. I told him instead of taking my website down and then announcing that my book and website were all false as he declared I must, I instead should rather install more stuff on it about how he banned me from attending my son's wedding.

Instantly he hit a nine on the rector scale for being uncivil. He yelled, "Don't put me on your website because I am just the messenger!" I told him OK, I will make sure my audience knows that. So now listen, everyone, apostle Steve Hargrave was only the messenger that banned me from my son's wedding! Readers, I repeat, don't accuse him of barring me from attending my children's wedding. He is only the messenger! Got it? Lol! A short time later, the same thing happened again concerning the demands I needed to comply with before allowing my presence at my son's wedding. Now my daughter was getting married. Once again, a little argument, and then I was banned and indirectly threatened with police involvement if I dared to show up! I can't believe that he wanted me to lie and announce that these true stories were a lie in order to attend both weddings! Demanding of me to be a liar! Is that a Godly demand?

Like already mentioned, but not really addressed, Danny Layne died several years ago. That is when things really started to change! Ray Tinsman became the leader. I think I met Ray when he was about twelve or thirteen years old. I was there when he preached his first message when he was about that age. He misplaced a Bible verse, and when he announced to the congregation his next verse, it wasn't there! He verbally stumbled around for a bit and finally moved on to his next verse. I have stayed at his parents' place, I think, more than once. I loved his family. His dad was a wonderful conversationalist and also a fantastic cook! His mother was adorable, and I heard she had died already. I loved the entire family. I enjoyed having Gerry Jr. (volleyball hernia) and Ray come up to Wisconsin the first time when it was about thirty below, straight temperature, not the wind chill factor, which was even worse!

Recently, I heard Ray has idolized a certain Country Singer and placed guilt upon his members for not being as famous. I only heard that. My focus is not on the singer, nor the popularity, but rather on the change that has taken place in the last twenty or thirty years! If a member was caught listening to this singer back in the mid-1990s, the member would have to get saved again at their altar and possibly even verbally apologize in front of the congregation for committing sin! But now it was esteemed!

The biggest and most disturbing change I have seen or heard is that they appointed themselves to be called "Apostles"! The other changes are irritating to me, but calling themselves this God-ordained term falsely, gives me godly indignation against them. That righteous anger propels me forward to write this book and explain why that is so wrong. I apologize now for possibly writing the next chapter with an aroma of hostility permeated within the pages. But please reason with the context, and see if it is not accurate to have extreme anger at how they rob and plunder that title wrongfully.

Ray Tinsman is known as the Chief of Apostle. I heard that they fleece from the congregations about three-quarters of a million dollars and then divide that amount among the apostles. I heard Ray gets about one hundred and fifty thousand dollars. Is it true that he received a forty thousand dollar bonus as his birthday gift? While some citizens struggle with ten or twenty grand a year, he lives pretty richly by being a leech off the members. However, I heard the church pays him indirectly by paying his bills, which makes the amount even greater if you avoid paying taxes on it. It sounds like laundered money! Is this also a form of extortion? Does the IRS know how it all happens? I heard all of this second-hand from people that were informing me of it all.

Concerning the false apostle Pat O'Shea, he moved to Ireland, across the ocean. I believe it was a slick move he had to make so that he could still be top cheese in his particular congregation. The Kenosha congregation shut down, so he either

40

had to go to some other pastor's congregation and only be the assistant pastor or move to where there isn't an established congregation. I believe Pat is not satisfied to be under the authority of anyone else. In Ireland, he isn't under the thumb of anyone like he would be if he had stayed in the States. Maybe he also needed to run from the identity I gave him with my first book.

When they use the term "Apostle" for themselves, it irritates me severely because I know what real apostles are supposed to be. I need to address this term with Biblical adrenaline and fury and with having God's hatred for them to claim it while they are **counterfeits.** Let us read the Book of Acts to see the difference! They have already admitted that if God led them to keep writing another chapter or more to the Bible, they believe it would be permissible according to their "self-righteous purity"! Disgusting!

CHAPTER NINE
REAL APOSTLE or
COUNTERFEIT?

*"For many shall come in my name, saying, I am Christ, and shall
deceive many."*
Matthew 24:5

Deception is running rampant when the leaders of a group
start giving themselves titles without having the substance to
support their claim. If Ray Tinsman is the Chief of the modern-day
apostle, then the group shouldn't be worried about comparing him
with the Apostle Peter or Apostle Paul, who were tremendously
used of God. So Cult members, please don't hate this chapter
because the comparison should be equal to Apostle Peter, at least
as good or even better than Peter, according to these false apostle's
beliefs or claims. Agree? So let us compare!

THE BOOK OF ACTS
Please follow in your Bible because I am not always going to type
each verse.

- **1:4** Jesus had personally been with the Apostles, including
  Paul, while on the way to Damascus. A counterfeit has
  never been literally & personally been with Jesus.
- **1:15** The real Apostles started with a group of about 120
  people.
- **1:26** Before these Apostles were filled with the Holy Spirit,
  they voted to replace Judas with Mathias. Very little is
  mentioned about him again. Isn't it unique, though, how,
  when God voted someone in, Apostle Paul was a miracle
  and nearly wrote most of the New Testament. Mathias was
  not a counterfeit but did as much as a modern-day
  counterfeit, nothing worth mentioning! Could it be that
  man appointed them into a position instead of God?

- **2:14** *"But Peter, standing up with the eleven, lifted up his voice..."*. A real Apostle steps forth and takes charge of the crowd with authority and preached Christ whom ye crucified! Counterfeits will preach for you to join their group instead of pointing to Christ.
- **2:32** Real Apostles have witnessed the risen Christ. Counterfeits have not.
- **2:36** Real Apostles will not cower or be timid by declaring, *"whom ye have crucified, both Lord and Christ."* Counterfeits will preach more about their group.
- **2:37** God's real Apostle will have the Holy Spirit on their side, which will *"pricked in their heart.."* of their audience. Counterfeits do not have that power and must use a lot of yelling and screaming to create fear. They need to control their followers by fear.
- **2:41** Real Apostles allow the Holy Spirit to work, which resulted in 3000 souls to convert to Christianity. Counterfeits can barely hang onto 3000 people (probably less) for forty years, which hardly ever grows in numbers. The only growth is when their members have babies.
- **2:43** Real Apostles had *"many wonders and signs done by the apostles."* Fake counterfeits have no signs and wonders, and when they declare someone will live, the victim dies!
- **2:44-45** Real Apostles had the people sell their goods and possessions, *"and had all things common;...and parted them to all men, as every man had need."* Counterfeit Apostles preach for their members to sell and bring them their goods, but then only heap the spoils upon themselves, the fake apostles!
- **2:46-47** Real Apostles had *"singleness of heart"* and *"the Lord added to the church daily..."*. Fake counterfeits do not have **daily** conversions, maybe not even monthly or yearly!
- **3:1-5** Apostle Peter and Apostle John healed a lame man! Counterfeit apostles don't have any power! They have NEVER performed INSTANTANEOUS healing ever! They commit blaspheme when they use the title of Apostle but

are powerless when compared to the Real Apostles that Jesus used.

- **3:6** Then the Real Apostle, Peter, *"said, silver and gold have I none; but such as I have to give I thee.."*. Usurping the God-given title of Apostle, the Counterfeit is the opposite of Peter. "Silver and Gold (about 150Grand per year) have I, but you don't get it. However, the healing power, well, sorry, I can't give it to you either, BECAUSE I DON'T HAVE IT! According to their claim, why they can't heal is because the lame man doesn't have faith. However, the Real Apostle did it in the name of Jesus, while the fake did it probably in the name of their apostle!

- **3:7** It was the faith and power of Apostle Peter that healed him, and NOT the faith of the lame man. The man thought he might get some money from them and knew absolutely nothing of what he was about to get. Peter had to reach down and, by his faith, pulled the lame man to his feet, and **immediately** he was healed. The counterfeit apostle does not have that power and blames it on the lame man because he only expected money. Did you ever wonder what would happen in the camp of the counterfeit apostles if one of their leaders got sick like apostle Gerry Jr. and suppose all the other apostles did the praying? Was it the sick man, apostle Gerry Jr.'s fault, or was it apostle "Whoever" that doesn't have faith if the sick man died? If there is such a thing that the sick person must have faith in order for the miracle to perform, then there would be several examples in the Bible of where Jesus or the Apostles could not heal. But it is ironic that in about (1986-9?), almost forty years, the counterfeit Apostles have never found even one person that had the faith to be healed **immediately**, even if it is their own apostle Mutch! One apostle praying for the next apostle, and they still can't make it work! The most obvious explanation is that their counterfeit apostles are the weak links of this faithless equation.

- **3:12** Real Apostles right away place the praise and credit on Jesus and remove it from themselves. Counterfeit apostles preach long messages praising their own apostles (that have no Spirit-filled power) and demand their followers to pray to them for healing and help. They claim Jesus casually so that if there ever is healing within the next hundred years, they can take the people's praise and keep it for themselves. Therefore, Jesus probably doesn't claim them. How can he claim them if they demonstrate ungodliness and wickedness? I believe I will have the Counterfeit apostle Reviler call me after this book is published and yell at me things that Jesus never would. They simply hate the truth.

One time I asked "apostle (joke)" Pat O'Shea to list the **immediate** healings that he ever was with or witnessed. He told me of one that was a miracle healing down in Chicago at a church he used to attend. Then he told me another one that he witnessed in the Faith and Victory group, also years earlier. I was impressed that my belief was reinforced, that God still can do miracles today! However, Pharisee Pat O'Shea got very angry with me when I pointed out that both those miracles were done in what he would call Babylon or the false churches. And now he couldn't tell me even one that happened in this One True Church? He was mad when I told him that. God, however, is still doing miracles today, except not in a self-seeking church.

- **3:15** Once again, God's Apostles witnessed the crucifixion and the resurrection! Counterfeits might be committing blasphemous statements by labeling themselves with that Godly title but do not have the attributes of an Apostle.
- **4:4** Real Apostles work for the Lord's church, and another 5000 were added to it. Fake apostles work toward adding numbers to their own church, which instead is shrinking. There used to be a congregation in Africa, but I heard it fizzled away. In fact, they for years tried stealing members out of God's church, which he built about 2000 years ago.

These Christians are worshiping in other congregations, so they trick them by twisting the scriptures to make them join their COGR with their own rules.

Here in **Acts**, there were 3000 new converts earlier, and now another 5000 conversions, which made the Lord's Church maybe 10,000 strong by now in a very short time. In contrast, the counterfeits in over thirty years might still be at 3000 worldwide and probably much less. Their women need to have more babies!

- **4:5-12** God's Apostles constantly gave the credit and praise to Jesus, and NEVER to themselves. Counterfeits steal any praise that belongs to God, preach arrogance to themselves, and expect salvation through them.

- **4:13** Even the Jesus hating Priests acknowledged that these Apostles had been with Jesus and therefore displayed the power of the one they crucified. In contrast, only their own cult members are deceived into believing that their weak counterfeit apostles had been with Jesus.

- **4:16** The Priests acknowledged the *"notable miracle,"* and they could not *"deny it."* In thirty years, the counterfeit apostles have yet to perform a notable miracle, which could not be denied, nor explained away as natural healing! Natural healing happens daily, even to a sick dog that gets up after three days and is healed. A miracle healing requires a Godly individual to be in harmony with God so that God can do the healing. The sick individual might not have faith or know anything about God. Probably most of the people healed in the Bible were sinners and non-believers, but the faith of the Apostle or Jesus raised them up. When does a sinner have faith to be healed? Extremely rare, or they probably would be saved if they had the faith. But evil apostles blame the lack of faith on their members as to why they can't perform a miracle.

- **4:17** The name of Jesus was the threat to the Priests, and that is what was forbidden for the Apostles to speak. But in the desolate camp of the confused, rarely did I hear the message of Jesus crucified and resurrection, and the only thing we need. Sure there were messages preached about hellfire if you don't follow them. I don't think I will ever forget the time a stranger came into our midst. She declared that she was saved and living for Jesus. The fake apostles and congregation were quiet. However, when after a while mentioned that she wanted to join this group, the place went wild. There was a lot of shouting and "Praise the Lord"- screamed comments made! It was ironic that when Jesus was mentioned, the place was quiet, but I took notice of it and felt it was wrong. Is that the real reason there are no miracles? I believe that.

- **4:19** God's Apostles "hearken" unto God, and do his will. Counterfeit apostles hearken unto the other fake leaders, whom they named apostles. That is blasphemous!

- **4:20** God's Apostles will answer, *"For we cannot but speak the things which we have seen and heard."* Unfortunately, for the fake apostles, they can't make that claim, but yet they hijack the title of "Apostle" wrongfully, claiming they are equal to God's Apostles. God's Apostles were movers and shakers in the New Dispensation. Only the deceived members quake and tremble from the voice of these counterfeit apostles. At the end of chapter four, Deuteronomy 18:20-22 is mentioned, which ends with the comment that a false prophet, *"thou shalt not be afraid of him."* They don't have any Godly power. However, they could kill you physically.

- **4:31** *"the place was shaken."* When God's people gather, God shakes the place. Before Elijah made his burnt offering, the heathen prophets of Baal worship were shaking the place up, cutting themselves and screaming loudly, and jumping on their altar,... yet with all that noise, nothing happened. Then Elijah spoke quietly, and God spoke loudly with fire, and the heathens trembled! Counterfeits make a loud show when they pray for a baby. There was a lot of man-made shaking when people beat their fists on the benches while they screamed to God to save the child. All that noise and pounding, and that baby died anyway! And they call themselves apostles? Oops! I overlooked the idea that the baby didn't have faith! Therefore, the apostles are not at fault, but it was the baby's lack of faith that forced it to die! Nonsense!

The counterfeits took the blame away from apostle Elizabeth and her vision of healing for the man that died because there was unbelief and doubt in the camp. It was because the members of the congregation had a lack of faith. Therefore, the man had to die! I find it ironic that all these doubters were NEVER present when Jesus or the Apostles did the miracles (sarcasm statement)! If there had been, would not we have examples of Jesus not being able to heal? Or were there doubters, sinners, and demon-possessed individuals that didn't have faith, but the faith of the **RIGHTEOUS** healed the sick? Counterfeit Apostles want to pass the blame so that they don't appear unrighteous. If the shoe fits so perfectly, why don't they wear it? The answer is scriptural, in that in the last time many false prophets (Apostles?) shall come and deceive many,... about 3000 or less, and shrinking?

- **4:32** The Godly Apostles had all the possessions, common – everyone's goods. The modern-day counterfeit apostle leeches the money from the congregation and members, and only their apostles enjoy the spoils. That is sick! Where are the thinkers left in their midst that can see that point? Don't they read their Bible anymore? The Bible I read commands, *"Seek out your own salvation with fear and trembling."* But the counterfeits must have a different distorted bible that must read, **"let your apostle seek out your salvation with greed and deception!"** Where are the serious thinkers that will understand the truth in scripture? Have they already left, and only the gullible remain? Why can't they see for what it really is?

Back to the heading of Chapter One. *"And with all*

*deceivableness of unrighteousness in them, that perish; because they received not the love of the truth, that they might be saved. And for this cause, **God shall send them strong delusion, that they should believe a lie"***. Wake up, cult members. Don't believe me. I was excommunicated from their presence and couldn't even attend two of my children's weddings. But please study your Bible and see if these things are true, or eternity will be harsh.

- **4:33** Cult members, when was the last time you heard a message that Jesus was the only thing you needed, the resurrection of the Lord Jesus? It is true, and yet the counterfeits add themselves as an additional need that is mandatory to get to heaven. Jesus is actually not as important as they are (paraphrased). What I heard is getting preached now among these counterfeits. Did you catch what apostle Rat Tinsman said about praying to Jesus? He called that weird stuff!

- **4:34-35** Repeat of what was already mentioned. The Bible Saints of the New Testament sold their lands and houses and laid them down at the Apostle's feet. However, the truth <u>DOESN'T</u> end there because the distribution took place after that to **ALL** the members of the new church, according to their needs. The hypocritical apostles preach the first half of this passage and take it out of context, **BUT** then live quite well by keeping the money for only the deceiving counterfeits. Three-quarter of a million dollars is disgusting to be hoarded by these powerless phonies! It would not be so appalling if they were just pastors like they were when I left them about twenty years ago. But since then, they took the title of apostle, and that is an abomination because they are not even close to resembling what God's anointed Apostles were like. Somebody needs to expose this crime since these counterfeits chose to burglarize that title, which is thievery if it doesn't belong to them. I pray that a few members in this bondage will see the truth of this hypocrisy. It is the abduction of the term

Apostle.

- **4:36** It takes a lot to be a Barnabas. However, he gave his entire possessions to God's anointed, not to thieves of the false titled counterfeits!
- **5:1-10** This was the passage that Danny Layne enjoyed often using to separate marriages wrongfully. According to scripture, though, it was demonstrating the power of the Holy Spirit and the discernment of an Apostle to look beyond the visual. If a cult member did the same today and brought a hundred grand to these counterfeits with claims it was all, the member would be protected and loved. Counterfeit men look on outward. God looks at the heart!
- **5:3** *"But Peter SAID..."*. Peter simply spoke quietly and stated the truth. No yelling was needed, no reviling! However, when members or outsiders like myself dare oppose these liars and thieves of God-given titles, animosity and yelling might follow. These counterfeits despise and HATE being challenged with the Word of God.
- **5:11** *"And great fear came upon all the church, and upon as many, as heard these things."* The real Godly Apostles created fear by exposing lies, which then the Holy Spirit killed the liars. In contrast, the counterfeits create fear by first twisting and using this scripture in tearing marriages apart by appealing to the deceived spouse that will submit to their lies. *"What God hath joined together, let no"* (counterfeit apostle) *"man put asunder."* The counterfeit apostles are just "men," and evil they are!
- **5:12** A miracle in the book of Acts just doesn't happen just once. It is repeated over and over again, often! So it repeats again, *"And by the hands of the apostles were MANY signs and wonders wrought among the people.."* Is there anyone that can name JUST ONE miracle that was done by these counterfeit apostles in the last thirty years? Take at least a dozen counterfeit apostles, multiply by 365 days a year, multiply that by 30+ years, and nobody can name EVEN ONE miracle which could not be explained away by natural

circumstances?

- **5:14** Even though Peter, a real Apostle, just demonstrated that he had discernment and used the Holy Spirit to kill any liar of it, the church numbers increased again. On the other hand, when the counterfeits excommunicate one of the spouses, they lose another member, which causes fear among the rest of their members to obey these counterfeits.
- **5:15** People started putting sick people on the roads where they expected Peter to walk, so his shadow of him might heal them. Who in their right mind would place a sick person near a counterfeit apostle that for thirty years could not instantly heal a single headache ever? But yet they demand to be called Apostle? Lunacy!
- **5:16** The counterfeit apostles work hard at placing the blame for why they can't heal on their followers. They claim that the members don't have the faith to be healed. In this verse, people brought a variety of individuals to be healed. Do you believe that the *"folk...vexed with unclean spirits"* had the faith to be healed, and if they didn't have the faith, do you believe that Peter would not have been able to heal them? Crazy thinking, which is an ungodly assumption.
- **5:18** When is the last time the counterfeit apostle was thrown in prison because they could perform a miracle while all the priests couldn't? Oh, yes, it doesn't happen! That's because a miracle has NEVER been performed in thirty years by any of them.
- **5:19** Angels of the Lord speak to Real Apostles, and even prison bars can't hold them in chains when God has a task for them to do.
- **5:**23 In this verse, it was another miracle how the Apostles got out of there with the prison door still shut and the guards still standing watch. The counterfeit apostles couldn't do that because they would blame the guards or the prison door for not having enough faith for these apostles to do that miracle. Someone or something gets the

51

blame, but not them! It could have been the locks that didn't have the faith, right? Fort Counterfeit has powerful locks!

- **5:26** God's Apostles get respect from authorities. Counterfeit apostles receive contempt.
- **5:29** *"We ought to obey God rather than men."* My desire is that this book might free some of these cult members to be able to say those words with conviction!
- **5:32** *"the Holy Ghost, whom God hath given to them that obey him."* That is the key to why some Real Apostles have power, and counterfeit apostles have no power. They do NOT obey God but are very carnal. Have you met apostle Reviler, apostle Deceiver, apostle Liar, and apostle Arrogant? I have, and they all deserve a small "a" for the title they have taken as hostage.
- **5:33** *"When they heard that* **(truth),** *they were cut to the heart, and took counsel to slay them."* It sounds like the verse is talking about the counterfeit apostle because they despise truth. But no, the verse is actually talking about some other people with the same spirit; the scribes, priests, and Pharisees. These people placed burdens on the people (members), which they themselves would not carry, nor could they perform the miracles that Peter was doing.
- **5:34-39** There might be a "Gamaliel" among the counterfeit apostles. God's warning is to flee, or else you will be judged with them.
- **5:39** *"But if it be of God, ye cannot overthrow it; lest haply ye be found even to fight against God"* Regardless if it is Balaam's donkey, the rooster that crowed three times, or a member that left because they saw error; if they speak God's truth, the counterfeit apostle will be fighting against the truth because they hate it. If the contents of this book are filled with Godly truth, it will stand, despite that they will fight against it.
- **6:1 & 7** When the true Word of God is preached, the new disciples multiply. In pathetic man-controlled groups, they

rarely grow very fast or with multiplied numbers. Almost forty years total from the beginning, and less than 3000 members worldwide, doesn't resemble the movement of real God-fearing Apostles. Are you part of that stale movement that doesn't hardly move?

- **6:8 all the way to 7:53.** The God-ordained "Apostle" Stephen in **Acts** (not Hardgrave) spoke the truth regardless of the dangers of even death. In contrast, counterfeit apostles will tell the authorities lies, deceptions, or simply what they want to hear so that their "hide" doesn't get in trouble! The question was, "Why didn't you call 911 sooner?" Real apostles would have told the truth regardless if there were consequences, even to the point of getting stoned! Pat O'Shea wouldn't have gotten stoned, but he was a liar, according to the very own message he preached. He was a deceiver that day!

- **7:60** Stephen had FALSE accusations against him, and in his dying breath said, *"lay not this sin to their charge."* In contrast, several of us are stating TRUE accusations against these counterfeit apostles. Different than godly people, this cult hates the truth and, in response, wishes and try to crucify the truth bearer! Even King David was kind to Shimei and even allowed him to continue to throw literal stones at David. I am not hurling literal stones, yet I believe the counterfeit apostles will attempt revenge against me.

- **8:1-4** Starting in **7:58,** Saul shows his appearance as a very evil man, starting to persecute the young church. Even though scattered, the Apostles and their members continued, *"everywhere preaching the word."* After reading this book so far, you can be assured that *"the word"* was not the preaching of joining their group but rather salvation in Jesus.

- **8:5-13** Amazing! Philip is mentioned here doing many miracles, healing, and casting out unclean spirits. Counterfeits would not be able to do that because the unclean spirits wouldn't have the faith to be cast out.

According to the fake apostle's claim, the faith of everyone present is a requirement for them to do a miracle, and that has never happened in thirty years! That is their excuse why they can't instantly heal even a headache. They claim that they have more faith than the early apostles. However, because the faithless people who want to get healed or because there are doubters in the audience watching, therefore, these hypocrites can't perform! Isn't it ironic that even the unclean spirits (according to this cult) must have had faith for Philip to cast them out? Also, notice that Philip and all the others mentioned in the Book of Acts never have a prefix title. But this group ALWAYS needs a prefix, "Brother" at the minimum, but even better now, "Apostle."

Notice this man, Simon, who is mentioned. He was a sorcerer and had used witchcraft before Philip arrived. Was he one of the people who had the evil spirit cast out because it states that he was converted? The counterfeits would not be able to cast the spirit of devils out. Worse yet, what if these counterfeits could cast out devils? Could these cult members then be the recipients of the demons, as it happened the time it went into the pigs instead, and they ran into the sea and drowned? Mt. 8:28-34. Jump ahead to **Acts 19:13-16.** Some counterfeit Jews (like Cult apostles) tried casting out devils. The powerless counterfeits were attacked by the devils, which they tried casting out. These men tried casting out these spirits by using these words, *"We adjure you by Jesus whom Paul preacheth"*...But the evil spirits responded, *"Jesus I know, and Paul I know; but who are ye?" And the man in whom the evil spirit was leaped on them, and overcame them, and prevailed against them so that they fled out of that house naked and wounded.* Casting out demons is a miracle, just like healing or opening prison doors is a miracle. Therefore, the fake apostles better hope they don't get caught up with a devil-possessed individual because the situation mentioned here

54

could happen to these counterfeits.

In Mark 9:17-19, a man came to Jesus and told him about his son, who had a bad spirit. Jesus's disciples couldn't cast the spirit out at that time. But in the book of Acts, they were no longer disciples, but they had become Apostles. They had graduated from the amateur level. These Cult Counterfeits are either amateurs or maybe they are not even disciples of Jesus! *"Ye shall know them by their fruit"*! The fruit that is displayed in the videos is worshipping a man, self-righteous fruit filled with blasphemous statements.

- **8:18** This Simon wanted to buy this power that real Apostles have. Apostle Peter rebuked him. The counterfeit apostles probably would take his money, but then how do you sell something that you don't possess yourself?
- **9:1- (15)** Saul was converted on the road to Damascus. God told Ananias, *"he* (Saul) *is a chosen vessel unto me, to bear my name."* Counterfeits CLAIM to be chosen, but in contrast, strive to bear their Chief Apostle Ray's name or their own.
- **9:22** Saul increased in strength, probably because he preached the *"very Christ."* What do counterfeits preach?
- **9:33-34** Eneas, sick of the palsy, Peter (doesn't need the prefix "Apostle," like the Cult covets!), and so *"Peter said unto him, Eneas, Jesus Christ maketh thee whole: arise,...".* Counterfeits say, in the "name of Ray"... That is blasphemous! That is the reason I was compelled to write this book and try to warn outsiders of this false doctrine. People that have left this cult are probably tormented and not thinking correctly spiritually. I hope they read this book to possibly bring healing.
- **9:40-42** Peter brought back a dead woman named Tabitha! She is alive again! Now let us look at it from a Counterfeit Apostles' perspective. Did you notice that Peter had to remove all the doubters from the room? (Sarcasm now) Would Peter have been able to do that if there were doubters present? The excuse the cult used why their

apostle Elizabeth made the false healing claim for the man, which is STILL DEAD, is because there was doubt in the congregation.

But this story leaves another problem for these blasphemous counterfeits. Only Peter and the DEAD Tabitha were in that room. However, the counterfeits would not be able to raise her back to life because her faith to be raised had perished. Therefore it wouldn't be these poor apostles' fault why they couldn't heal her back to life. It's because her faith was dead!

- **10:25-26** Listen to the first "youtube" again, which I listed at the beginning of this book, and find the place where their apostle is talking about this story about Cornelius. They did like verse 25 but totally ignored verse 26. Why? Because it goes against their doctrine. Cornelius bowed down and worshipped Peter. The story isn't finished! In the next verse, Peter pulled him back on his feet and said, *"I myself also am a man."* That is Godly humility. Peter didn't exalt himself nor let anyone else exalt him. Watch the video how these counterfeit apostles lavish the exaltation and the praise of men. (Sarcasm now!) Oh, yes, that is right, these apostles have more knowledge, understanding, or wisdom than those Apostles had that Jesus knew!

    Even Jesus must not have had the wisdom (sarcasm) of accepting the praise of men like their Chief Apostle Ray Tinsman has. Jesus is definitely good, but when somebody called him *"Good Master,"* Jesus responded, *"Why callest thou me good? There is none good but one, that is God"..* Jesus and the true Apostles are humble and refuse titles and exaltation. How many times can you find in the Bible where the title "Apostle" is the prefix before the name? In my Bible, I see a lot of Peter, James, and John: but I don't recall seeing "Brother Peter" or "Apostle Peter" used much. Jesus never used those titles. Does this cult have more light than God in the flesh?

- **10:34-35** *"Then Peter opened his mouth, and said, Of a* *truth, I perceive that God is no respecter of persons: But in every nation, he that feareth him, and worketh righteousness, is accepted with him."* Is that verse false because it is contrary to the cult's belief that their leaders need to approve if that believer can go to heaven? Nonsense!

- **12:1-16** King Herod killed the Apostle James with a sword. He also arrested Peter and threw him in prison with four sets of four guards, two of them chained to Peter with two chains. But there were real Apostles praying. An angel woke up Peter, and the chains fell off Peter's hands. Peter didn't even believe what was happening and thought it was a vision.

- Nevertheless, he followed the angel out of prison, past the sixteen guards, and then the big iron gate surrounding the prison, opened by God's unseen power! As soon as he was past the first street, the angel suddenly disappeared! Peter made haste and went to Mary's house, where the real people of God were praying. Peter knocked on the door, and Rhoda heard Peter's voice and knew it was him but didn't open the door. She ran back inside and told the others. The congregation that were praying didn't have faith and didn't believe Rhoda. They accused her, *Thou art mad."* and *"It is his angel."* But Peter kept knocking, and then they saw the truth!

  Now counterfeit apostles constantly blame the lack of faith on the congregation, of why they (these magnificent apostles which they claim they are) don't have the power to heal. So if one of them were in prison, let us assess and number all the faithless obstacles in the way. They need to place the blame on someone, or something else, for why they can't do miracles.

1. The two chains, which were locked onto Peter's wrists, didn't have any faith!
2. The two sleeping guards chained to Peter didn't have any faith!

57

3. All sixteen guards didn't have any faith!
4. The locked prison door didn't have any faith!
5. The big iron gate and its huge lock didn't have any faith!
6. Even Peter thought it was a vision!
7. Rhoda kind of believed, but not enough to take action! Just inadequate faith!
8. The people praying didn't have faith and ridiculed Rhoda!
9. Therefore, you can't blame the cult apostles for not being able to do miracles.

And yet God used the humble Apostles whom he chose and did miracles with them BECAUSE they continued to preach Jesus. Counterfeit apostles preach about themselves and their excuse for no miracles, and it is because there are so many faithless locks, guards, and people! I wish their members would just ponder on the idea that just maybe, why their apostles can't do miracles is because God doesn't perform miracles for the people that are self-righteous, striving to build their own agenda.

- **12:21-23** King Herod, adorned in fine clothing, made a big speech, and the people shouted, *"It is the voice of a god, and not of a man."* Immediately, an angel of the Lord struck him dead *"because he gave not God the Glory: and he was eaten of worms, and gave up the ghost."* After you have listened to the first two videos, do you think these apostles are deflecting all man praise and give God the praise?
- **13:11** Saul's name was getting changed to Paul, and he struck an evil man, a sorcerer, blind for fighting against the *"right ways of the Lord."* This cult would love to strike people like me blind, but we have nothing to fear. The reason is that this also was a miracle, and these counterfeits don't have any miracle power! If I was fighting against God's Church instead of Ray's church, I would be scared writing this book. But then, if they were the true church, then there wouldn't be any scriptures to contradict what they were doing.

The pattern is established in what the early Apostles did. They did a lot of miracles, and there were a lot of souls saved, and the real church grew! It grew with or without persecution and continued to increase every month. The Apostles were humble and refused a title in front of their name. They rejected to receive the glory and praise upon themselves but instead directed it to God. We only got to chapter 13 and then mentioned only one verse in chapter 19. So much is already mentioned, illustrating the overwhelming amount of miracles the Apostles did. It is not necessary to continue in hopes of finding more proof that these Counterfeit cult pastors have wrongfully stolen an identity title that doesn't belong to them. You can continue reading the rest of the book and see the same type of miracles and movement as these first chapters have displayed. Let us outline this chapter.

Comparison! Summary!	

Real Apostles were with Jesus	Counterfeits were never with Jesus
MANY miracles	Not EVEN ONE miracle in 30 years!
Thousands were converted at a time	Almost no converts, except their children. They need more babies!
Church grew fast	Stagnant, if not shrinking
Very humble Apostles	Arrogant, prideful apostles
Peter was never called by Prefix title	Mandatory title- "Brother" or apostle
Deflected praise, refused it	Lavishes Praise of men, encourages it
Preached "Jesus alone."	Preach, "they, themselves"
Donated $, distributed to ALL	Counterfeits hoard for themselves

CHAPTER TEN
BATTLE AGAINST EVIL

"For we wrestle not against flesh and blood, but against
principalities, against powers,
against the rulers of the darkness of this world,
against spiritual wickedness in high places.
Ephesians 6:12

My children, who are in this cult that have these counterfeit apostles, have warned me of a certain man that is crazy. They described him as some lunatic that is extremely fanatical in behavior. I heard the causes commotions on Sunday mornings that even Police officers needed to be called to keep the peace! This man is getting a following, and some Sunday mornings, there might be twenty or thirty people standing across the street of their chapel and yelling obnoxious things. My children told me if I ever had anything to do with that nut case, that they would withdraw from me and not speak to me. I had that warning given to me; I think it was already a few years ago. How he was described, I assumed he must be quite strange for having big banners and billboards plastered to his pickup truck. They told me he was in trouble with the law and has been in jail for doing these stupid demonstrations. I wouldn't reach out to somebody with that kind of reputation, and I never did. My reputation was too important to me to be hanging around and be seen with a "crazy man."

About that time when I heard of him, my son was getting married. That is when I was called by the infamous apostle Steve! I remembered him from when I had been at his mother's house for the weekend. It was a joy to talk to him until he placed demands on me in order to attend my son's wedding. He told me I MUST take my website down. I didn't design or install it and would not know how to take it down unless I went back to my web designer. Steve then said, could I instead add a letter to that website, that the

61

website and my book are all false and that I was mistaken? I objected by saying all the stories in the book are true. I asked if he had read it, and he told me no, and that he had no intentions of ever doing that. He then asked me to give an example of what I call true. So, I elaborated on how my ex-wife intentionally lied to the police about how I supposedly grabbed her wrists. It was a lie!

He then told me my story was not true because it was only how I perceived it! Wow! I don't know if it is sunny out today or if it is raining? Just because I perceive it that way doesn't mean it is true according to his interpretation! And here is an apostle that is demanding that I lie about all my true stories and experiences; I should call them false? Then about a year later, it was a repeat when my daughter's wedding came along. I told him instead of taking things down. I should add to the website how he barred me from my own children's wedding. Instantly he was not a quiet talking individual! "Don't put me on your website," he yelled. "I am just the messenger!" Now, readers, I heard he is the second in the authority of all the apostles. Do you think that with that kind of status and hierarchy or rank; do you really believe, he was <u>ONLY</u> the messenger? But I don't want to accuse him that he lied about having a say in this also, so I repeat what he told me, "he is only the messenger"! You decide.

Now, this last year, I mentioned that I have a new granddaughter, born at only one pound and twelve ounces! After several months later and several pounds added, I finally got to meet her. She is so cute! Smiling and all, it was an enjoyment to spend a few hours with her. However, when our meeting ended, my daughter followed me to my car and unloaded her disgust with me. I am continually trashing her friends in her cult. I told her I had not added anything on either the website or write another book for over a decade. She told me to take everything down, regardless of whether it was current. I told her no, and then she told me that she wanted nothing to do with me. She will not allow her daughter in the presence of grandpa, who trashes her friends.

I tried calling, and she didn't pick up. I texted, and no response. That is when I sent a letter stating that the only bargaining chip she has is used up if she doesn't respond. I have been holding back from writing more on the evils of this cult for more than a decade. I can't talk or communicate with them if I don't write, nor could I communicate with them if I do write again. So, what would I lose if I started writing again in hopes of waking up one lost soul in their midst?

It was then that I decided to write, but I have been unplugged for almost fifteen years and have limited information, not enough for a book. Therefore, I was searching for new developments. I thought about the lunatic, the mad man that my children were talking about. I needed to consider what kind of a fanatical character he was and list the things he was accused of:

1. He was hated by the cult and by my children. But I realized I was in the same boat. They hated me also, and unless I take my website down and then become a liar by claiming all the true stories were lies, I will not see my granddaughter again.

2. This Adam guy is voicing his opinion against what he sees in the cult. Once again, I understood that I was in the same boat. I have a website and a book and now writing a second book about them.

3. Yes- true, but he goes crazy by placing big signs and banners on his vehicles! My mind thinks about the time when I needed to take a four-foot-high by eight-foot-long plywood sheet, and I mounted it on both sides of my vehicle with things about the corrupt Kenosha court system. I had my dad weld a big fin sign that reached across the complete length of my fifteen-passenger van, high up across the top. It had my website address with at least a twelve to fourteen-inch-tall lettering, "screwedkenoshastyle.com," written across it. I must be a lunatic also! On the big plywood sign mounted on the side of my van, "Judge approves beating children with sawed-off golf clubs, and doesn't call that child abuse!" I am in the same boat again!

4. But this man had to get the police called on him. Strange

63

that my wife had falsely accused me, and I was arrested for that and hauled away in the police car. Once again, in the same boat!

5. But this Adam was in jail. But so was I falsely for an accumulated time of one full year! I started thinking that maybe this lunatic was a description of me! Isn't the definition of "fellowship" mean "more than one fellow in the same ship?" My children were describing me!

6. But this man does an obnoxious amount of picketing and demonstrations with signs. I then started thinking about the emotional terror that I started with, but then turned out to be exhilarating after the initial approach. I bought a black & white striped jail suit. Then I took a twelve-inch styrofoam ball and painted it black, and then wired it to a plastic chain and tied it to my wrist. I put my uniform on, and with large picket signs, I walked the Washington, DC political area. I walked around the United States Capitol, the United States Supreme Court, and the other buildings where our politicians have their offices. After that, my Judges started to recuse themselves from my case since I was a lunatic, for which my children gave the definition for! I have never been in jail since. It was worth it, and I would do it again, even worse if I needed to!

7. I still have not met this man, but I started to look at the truths he was writing about. He has a lot better skills than I do when it comes to modern technologies. On his different platforms or websites, he installed many of the cult's sermons and such. I started looking at them.

8. So, I challenge you to go into your kitchen, reach into your cupboard, and take the largest bag of salt you have. You probably used up one bag already while reading this book and my website! Now go to your computer and check out some of these sites, and with a little bit of salt -you will find some truth! But then, I am not being completely honest because this Adam guy simply recorded the cult's sermons (which have lies and false statements in them) and then

installed them on his various platforms. So if you want to know things about the cult from both sides of the aisle, there is one verse for you:

"Beloved, believe not every spirit, but try the spirits whether they are of God:
because many false prophets are gone out into the world." 1 John 4:1

- **cultbusters.us**
- **Facebook – Adam Pamer**
- **Facebook- Church of God cultbusters (over a 1000 members)**
- **YouTube, cultbusters**

I need to explain what I mean by the salt. Jesus talked about salt also. Food without any salt usually tastes blander. Salt brings out the flavor and also makes you thirsty for more. However, if a person puts too much salt on it, it is disgusting. As you read this book, I figured you would need to apply a little salt just so you can stomach my writing. Because the book has many chapters, you will go through a lot of salt. Therefore, I said you will need a large bag of salt to see everything that this Adam man installed because he has a lot of information, which I still haven't seen at all. I wrote this paragraph out of sarcasm. But on the serious side, I do hope, though, that this book and his various websites will be a help to you.

My children, I am sorry that you feel offended at me for trying to seek the truth. But I am not sorry for checking out some of the information above. And no, to what you are thinking; I still haven't met this man. However, I pray that you would take your Bible and search if there is no truth in this book and in the sites that this Adam lunatic man provided. I don't want you to scream on your deathbed as I heard a rumor about what one of your favorite pastors did when he was dying! I am striving to check out that rumor if that was so!

CHAPTER ELEVEN
WHY LIGHT THE FUSE?

I know there will be repercussions for writing this book. It is like lighting the fuse of a stick of dynamite. There will be an explosion, with an alteration of the environment. Some of my children will hate me and then disown me. They will avoid me in every way possible. I might get a call from apostle Reviler, and he will scream at me. There might be a lot of unseen ramifications which I haven't even thought of yet. So why am I so compelled to write this book? It is extremely important that I do, and let me explain why I should and did.

1. **It will not change the cult**. I know the cult's leaders, these counterfeit apostles, which will not change and become righteous just because I wrote this book. They will hate me for it, but they will not change. However, they will threaten all their members to shun me and warn their members about this book. If a member buys this book secretly and then gets caught with it, they will automatically be cast out of their church, condemned, and declared hell-bound. So why did I write it?

2. **Not for false doctrine**. I did not write it simply because they have some false doctrine. Look at the real Apostles before Jesus was crucified. They didn't comprehend what would take place, even though Jesus told him that he must die. They had a certain understanding that was blurred like, *"For now we see through a glass, darkly; but then face to face...".* So even the Apostles that had been with Jesus didn't see things exactly as God saw them.

   Therefore, I know that I don't have everything right according to the way that God sees things. What I think a certain scripture is saying might be different than what God meant. So hypothetically, if some people say "stepping on ants" is a wrong, ungodly, or even a sin; I wouldn't feel like attacking that topic because it doesn't have an eternal consequence if someone believes that or not. There are a LOT of topics like that, which are not eternal destination issues. So why did I write this book?

3. **Blasphemous doctrine!** The first reason for writing this book is the need to attack the blasphemous statements spoken in the first two videos. When somebody is beyond false doctrine and speaks blaspheme against the early apostles, that these phonies are better than they are, I get angry. That is blaspheme when Rat Tinsman said that praying to Jesus is weird stuff. It is blasphemous to demand people that are weary not to go to Jesus, but they need to go to Rat Tinsman. Statements like that need to be addressed with a God-filled hatred.

4. **Innocent, deceived members.** The second reason for writing this book is to hopefully get this book into the hands of the deceived members of this cult. If they can read it, maybe they will see the truth and get out. They need to flee this bondage of blasphemous doctrine.

5. **To the nightmare individual.** I was one! At the beginning of this book, I wrote about how I still had horror-filled dreams, of how I must have left God's holy church. I was somewhat a pioneer in finding some stable ground, with a method to walk on it, after I was ejected by this cult. Most people that leave or get excommunicated by this evil group of people lose out spiritually so far to the opposite side that they are doomed. Doomed in how they look or try to think. No hope, nearly suicidal. I had nightmares, and so did others.

I hope a book like this could be read by them to give them hope that they can trust Jesus without going to, or through, these counterfeits to make heaven. If just one aimless wandering soul could find peace in reading this book, my efforts would be paid in full! If you know a past member, or maybe it is you, please allow the various chapters which are Bible-based bless you. The points mentioned are what allowed me to pull out of the downward tailspin and the inevitable crash. If it helps someone, it will all be worth it, and that is the purpose of why I wrote it.

6. **The General Public.** I grieve to think these evil people are constantly trying to capture new victims into their system. On the outside, they look respectable and seem so pure. An honest, seeking soul might get the urge to visit their chapel. If they do, they will be showered with a lot of attention and fake love. The rules will be hidden from them until after they have joined and more time has elapsed. That is only when the torment begins. Therefore, the fourth reason for writing this book is to warn the public. Everyone NEEDS to know everything about these evil people, what they believe, and what they do. They should not be blindsided like I was when I first met them, and then after the fallout, all the malarkey and hostility I had to go through. Inform the public of the truth is my fourth reason.

7. **Easily available**. If it is complicated to get the information you need, it then quite often doesn't happen. If all the information is on the computer, the deceived member might not be able to get the information needed to escape the system. The cult has power over its members by not allowing them computer access with their phones. However, if this book was at every grocery store, convenience store, lumber yard, etc..., a cult member might look both ways to check if any other cult member is present and then buy the book secretly to get the truth. That is the mission, to make it available to everyone, and therefore, it has to be a book, which is my fifth purpose.

TORN ASUNDER IN THE JAWS OF A CULT

VOLUME 2

BY

BERNARD TOCHOLKE

DEDICATION

To the many shattered lives that were affected by the cult. To all the fathers, mothers, children who are and will always be affected by the experiences of this and all the other cults out there....
This book is also dedicated to Randy and David, my two sons that were with me from the beginning. I also want to thank everyone that helped me edit this book.

CHAPTER 1
MY DESIRE FOR THIS BOOK

This book is my feeble attempt to protect other people from becoming victims of a cult. I wish I could present my devastated experience in a way that will give you as the reader the knowledge you need to prevent the destruction of your marriage or family.

A person might boast that they will never be deceived by a cult. But, what can a person say to their spouse, children, parents or close friends when they start getting involved with a strange group? Do they have the wisdom to steer them away from something that will mar them for life or even cause them to die needlessly?

My desire for this book is to display how humanity gets sucked into cults, the exposure of this particular cult, and hopefully show ways to save a person and their loved ones from falling into a cleverly laid scheme.

The disgusting thing about cults is that the people who are involved or are getting involved actually believe they are doing the right thing. With sincerity, they believe the things that seem so strange to us. Yet it is nearly impossible to persuade them from their belief.

There are similarities between a person dying of hypothermia and someone caught up in a cult. When a body is first exposed to the cult or the cold, there is a resistance to this foreign thinking or confrontation. As for regarding the cold temperature, a body must resist the force of bringing their body temperature down. Shivering and teeth chattering is the beginning of the transition to hypothermal death. That step of the process toward death is actually the only painful feeling the body experiences. In a matter of minutes the victim's thoughts of cold changes to believing that he is actually warm. Once that condition has developed the body will die unless someone else takes the necessary action to recover this person from his definite doom. Even then it takes extreme medically related actions to bring the near statistic back to so called normality.

The term "so called normal" is exactly what it is. A person that has gone down that path of hypothermia or frozen body parts will for his remaining life have a weakness for the cold. Let us suppose a person had frozen his ears. Before that time he could easily tolerate temperatures well below freezing and never had a problem with his ears. However, when he overexposed the ears and froze them there is a change. He no longer has a resistance to the cold as he did before that instance. For many victims of frostbite, just a cool temperature can become painful. I heard heatstroke appears to have the same characteristics. Once a person has had a heatstroke, the conditions of heat and dehydration can be a lot milder and he could get another stroke.

Becoming a victim of a cult has a lot of the same similarities. When the first exposure comes, the body will resist the new concept of beliefs and practices. If the cult is clever it will reveal the rules slowly. As involvement takes place the body undergoes adjustments. Similar to hypothermia, some new rules might make a person's teeth chatter and also make his body uncomfortable. However, while staying in it even though you are having the effects of "cult" hypothermia, the body will soon move over to the danger zone of not feeling any harm or threat. At that point the downward spiral into doomed finality in this cult is definite.

I must mention also to one more danger about the tactics of this particular cult, which I am sure is also in other cults, is that people desire to strive for two things that make them vulnerable to the predator features of the cult. One human need is the desire for acceptance and praise of others. This cult will give the new members plenty of that. The main leader preached and taught it from the pulpit at how his listeners must approach the new members and visitors.

He demanded that we go out of our comfort zone to contact, honor, praise, help, encourage, embrace and befriend all new "seekers" of the truth. Nobody else has it. Now I am getting ahead of myself and will continue this thought later.

The second point of what people crave or strive for is this life-long mental struggle of trying to find God in their minds and to create a decision of how they view Him and His requirements. I do not intend to make this book a religious Bible study type of book. However, cults usually have a religious twist to them that captivates people's minds and victimizes them by their vulnerability for their quest in heavenly answers, truth, and purpose.

Find some correct truth, distort it slightly, then convince others to agree with it and there begins the foundation of a cult. However, the structure must follow this process or else it is just a foundation which is no more than a bad idea. The structure must have several criteria in it to actually become a cult. I hope this book will give you an understanding from someone that was a member of a cult. I was that man that was deceived. It cost me nearly everything to escape.

My desire is to share my hindsight 20/20 vision to protect you and your loved ones from paying the price that I had to pay to be revived from this spiritual or cult hypothermia. This might be a different cult than the one you might encounter. However, many characteristics will be the same.

In medical emergency rooms, bright lights, total open exposure with visual magnifying instruments is a must for intricate surgery. May this book be the bright light and exposure with visual aide to amputate the "cancer" from among us.

Please learn from my experience as I expose the hidden issues, rules, and things that have happened. The greatest thing you can do in return is if something emotionally stirred you in this book is to keep sharing the information to others. I want to thank you in advance for that.

Victim of Fury

The pastor (Patrick O'Shea) with his face red was yelling at me.
I leaned back against the wall as I watched him spend his fury.
"You think you will get the children?" he yelled," you will not get
the children! Shereen is going to get the children. You know it is a
woman's State".

My mind was racing fast at all the events that led up to this.
Now, I was facing the anger of the pastor whom I had at one time
called the leader of my family. My stomach was in a knot
preparing to jump up out of my throat. My legs were threatening to
collapse from underneath me.

"I had tried to save your marriage, but it is over! You will lose
your family. You will lose your business. You will lose your health.
You will lose your house and everything you love. You will lose
everything!" he screamed.

"You might think that you can convince your oldest two boys to
go with you, however, they will leave you too! They will turn
against you. You will be alone. You will die a miserable death. And
then you will have to meet God in your sinful condition. You will
be lost in hell.... for eternity! Is that what you want? As you have
defied the Church, you have done it unto God."

It might have been well over a half hour that he stood before me
just yelling with that red faced fury. The entire time his pointer
finger was stabbing the air a foot in front of my face. I felt sick
beyond description wondering if any of what he was saying was
true and could happen. That thought disappears as the spittle of this
pastor hits my shirt. With all this screaming he did not even notice
that he was venting his spit upon me too!

"Until you get some real serious spiritual help, Shereen will
need to leave you", was the conclusion of his confrontation against
me. I was mentally devastated thinking that the inevitable situation
had finally come to full term. Even though I could feel this
condition approaching at least two years earlier, denial of this exact

circumstance is so human. Even now I am still in denial or shock to fully comprehend what had been established by this angry pastor.

How did I get to this position where a pastor had the power to break up my marriage? Also, what had I done that was so vile, for him to destroy Shereen's and my marriage? My mind drifted back over the years to search for the answer to all my questions.

NOTE: Throughout the rest of the book I might refer to myself as "Bernie". It is the name I have been called since my youngest childhood days that I can remember which even continues until now.

CHAPTER 2
CRITERIA OF A CULT

The word cult conjures images of bodies covering the ground of Jonestown, blazing buildings in Waco, Texas, or the crazed eyes of Marshall Applewhite, leader of the Heaven's Gate cult. But what does it take to be a cult? According to the model developed by Robert J. Lifton there are eight criteria when determining whether or not a group can be classified as a cult.

1. Milieu Control
The word milieu is French, meaning surroundings or environment. A totalistic cult controls the environment of the congregation. In the case of the CoGR. (Church of God Restoration), members were told how to decorate their homes, what kinds of cars to drive and what types of entertainment were considered appropriate. A friend of mine, (we will refer to as E.R.) and a former member and co-founder of www.churchofgodrestorationexposed.us. posts this, "No listening to the radio, watching TV, or listening to unapproved music, even though there is one very odd allowance to the unapproved music part. People who sing specials in the services are allowed to listen to all the contemporary Christian music they want in order to find and learn new songs. It is assumed that anyone who is a special singer is so spiritual that they wouldn't be tempted by the worldliness in the songs."

Members are also discouraged from spending extended periods of time with their "unsaved" family for fear that they may influence the member negatively. Unsaved is everyone that does not attend this particular cult. If the relative goes to another church closely resembling the CoGR church, the restrictions against them are usually even more.

"When Danny Layne, out of California, first started the CoGR, many of the children attended public schools and a few home schooled their children. Eventually, home schooling became the rule. Around 1997 the church began running the illegal private schools by the ministry, further separating the members of the CoGR from the outside world. Most of the ministry-run schools have no certified teacher, which is a requirement for a private school, in Wisconsin anyway, making it illegal. The certified teacher part is not required for homeschooling. Therefore the parents will sign papers with the State that they are homeschooling but actually they will private school secretly.

2. Mystical Manipulation

In the CoGR the Holy Spirit is said to decide major occurrences within the church, when indeed it is the ministers who have the control. "They allow or disallow certain emotional outbreaks by the way they "Amen" members special singing, praying or testifying, or by their reaction to a certain preacher or certain message. (either positive or negative). If the ministers do not approve of a certain member being an active participant in the service they will "sit on them" meaning they will not "Amen" them, giving the clue to the rest of the congregation on how to act towards that member. By this method they make it seem that the Holy Spirit is working in a certain way." (from E.R.'s article on Mystical Manipulation).

Bernie experienced this often. To him it seemed ironic at how different members and visitors were treated. It seemed that the main leader, Danny Layne, believed that he had just the right balance of outward demonstration or expression of spirituality. When individuals and groups don't raise their hands or shout out "Amen" in the middle of songs or sermons, they are considered spiritually dead. Danny referred to several congregations or "Churches", as being the lifeless and dead churches. In one sermon of his, Danny preached that one certain church should have been called The Church of the Frigidaire (frigid air).

However, if someone came in their group that was more outgoing with his words and actions, he was condemned also as being charismatic in the evil sense of the word. He was considered as having a demonic spirit. It was confusing to see why that was considered wrong compared to Layne's behavior at other times. He is an older man but yet when he felt he needed to perform, he would jump, leap and run around shouting as he moved around the congregation in that service.

3. Demand for Purity

The group becomes obsessed with working towards purity. It became a monotonous repeat of testimonies as the "dedicated" members would at every prayer meeting repeat their same testimony that they gave last week or the week before at how they are dying to the flesh and to themselves. They usually repeat that they are glad that they are in the ONE, TRUE CHURCH! They might also praise God for taking them out of Babylon, which is any other church that is not CoGR.

The totalistic cult has a black and white view of the world. A person is either a sinner or they are saved. If they are not immersed in this church, they are not saved. There is no bending or meeting in the middle. The cult members might argue against this point that is being made here. Could some member of another church, please ask them if someone outside of their group could be saved, and they would probably answer, yes! However, don't stop there. Ask them if that person could remain in the other church, that they don't have any intention of leaving the other church to join their Church Of God (church/cult), and if that person then could still be saved? The answer then is, No!

4. The Cult of Confession

Any sins, as defined by the cult, are to be confessed immediately before the congregation and definitely the ministers. This becomes a way of solidifying the feeling of oneness needed in a cult.

In the CoGR, members have few secrets from the ministers or at least are not supposed to. With altar calls being made three times a week, members are encouraged to confess not only their own sins, but those of others as well. It goes so far as children reporting on parents and one spouse on the other which is very common. Ministers keep a file for each member of their congregation and note every confession, which is as a way to remind the confessor at a future date of his past failings.

5. The Sacred Science

This method prevents too many questions from being asked. The cult introduces its ideology as being absolute and unassailable. Any questioning of the doctrines of the CoGR is considered a sin. Anyone considering other points of view should repent immediately. The CoGR considers any questioning of their ideology to be questioning God Himself, as their belief is that they are the voice of God on earth today. (I will tell you of that very same rule that I broke.) I dared to question their doctrines and beliefs and am now paying the price for it. The main man, Danny, preached before all the pastors at a ministers meeting for them to root out the "free thinkers", "We don't need them. Get rid of them!" So eventually I was weeded out but lost my wife and children that are still with them.

6. Loaded Language

Lifton describes "thought terminating clich'es," as certain phrases used by the cult to instruct the listener on how to feel about a controversial subject. Within the CoGR there are many such phrases.

They use the words Babylon, The Beast, and The False Prophet which are all to describe all other churches besides them. The Catholic Church is regarded as being the Mother Harlot mentioned in Revelation. However, ALL other Bible based religions are regarded as the daughters of this Mother Harlot. Even if the church names itself the Church of God, if it does not fellowship with this CoGR group, it still is considered a daughter of this Mother Harlot and therefore also Babylon. All religions are wrong except theirs, and they will be destroyed.

The words Saved and Unsaved have a special meaning within the CoGR, no other meanings will do. Getting Unsaved is easy; it can happen at any time by merely disagreeing with them. They hold all of the control of whether or not your soul is worthy of heaven.

7. Doctrine Over Person

The doctrine of the cult is held higher in regard than the people experiencing it. The history of the group can be changed to fit the doctrinal needs of the cult. A person's value is determined by how well he serves the cult. In the CoGR, people have literally died for the doctrine. Parents have refused their children medical treatment, resulting in death, and adults have refused their own care. There are some inconsistencies which I will mention later.

8. Dispensing of Existence

This is the criteria in which the leaders of the cult decide who is fit to exist and who is not. Members are cut off from their families and other outsiders. The leaders of the cult determine which books are accurate and which are not. People who were once members of the CoGR are railed against in a far harsher manner than those who were never "Saved". The offending member is ex-communicated sometimes in a formal letter. Pauletta desired to court a man that was not part of the CoGR. She also desired to work at a job that the founder of this cult, Danny Layne, refused to give permission to work at. Because of reasons like that, she was pronounced "Unsaved" and condemned by the ministry. I was there when Danny preached her condemnation from the pulpit. We were ordered to avoid her like a contagious disease. We were told about excommunicated individuals, that if we see them coming down the sidewalk, we should quickly cross to the other side of the street. If we do not, the same judgment will fall on us.

Pauletta received a formal letter with the CoGR letterhead. Danny Layne along with four other ministers signed it. Two of the ministers, were her own two brothers. In this letter she is told "This Sentence of excommunication or banning will last until you are dead". She was "cut off", considered as "dead", and also denounced as being turned over to Satan. The letter also decreed that anyone within the CoGR who is found to be talking or associating with Pauletta would suffer the same fate. She was restricted or banned from being able to attend any of their church functions including any gatherings for weddings or funerals, even if it is of her own blood family. A few years later her brother died and she was barred from attending that funeral. He was one of the five ministers that had signed her excommunication letter. On my website, www.screwedkenoshastyle.com , you can find a copy of the letter she received.

The Church of God Restoration (CoGR) meets and exceeds all of the eight criteria set forth in Robert J. Lifton's model.

In February, 2007, in response to the launching of my friend's website www.churchofgodrestorationexposed.us , exposing them as a cult, the ministry posted an article on its own website. In the article titled "What is a cult?" the group uses biblical references to justify its meeting the criteria that makes it a cult. For each of the thirty-five points listed in the article, Bible verses are taken out of context in order to support the idea that being a cult is what is ordered by God.

CHAPTER 3

THE GRADUAL EXPOSURE OF THE RULES

There is a great danger in this area of topic. The group does not expose all their beliefs to their new visitors or members right away. There is no list that you can obtain with all their strange beliefs and doctrine. The exposure to the rules requires time, but once a point is addressed, the new member receives a little time to "measure up". If sufficient time goes by without the new member accepting the change, he could be labeled suddenly as "Unsaved" even though he didn't commit any other sin besides not measuring up to the "new light".

If you ask Patrick O'Shea if the Church of God Restoration imposes any rules on his congregation he will likely answer "I don't believe in rules. If people want to follow church teachings, they want it and if they don't, they don't," as was his response in a Kenosha News article dated April of 2003. (Also posted on my website). However, if a member "chooses" not to follow the rules, he will likely no longer be welcome as a member of the Church of God Restoration. The rules, unwritten or otherwise, impinge on every aspect of the CoGR member's life. The list comprises regulation on everything from the clothing worn to the types of family entertainment members are allowed to participate in.

The women of the CoGR carry the responsibility of never tempting the men of the church with their bodies. To meet the CoGR;s standard of modesty, a woman must wear four layers of clothing. She has to wear a bra and panties, which must be only white color cotton, with no extra design lace or any adornments of any kind. Over this she wears a full slip, also with no decorative lace or embroidery. This layer is covered by a long sleeved, button down shirt, with a collar. The shirt must be buttoned to the very top. It was preached from the pulpit that the "top button will keep your daughter from having an abortion." On her bottom half she wears an ankle length skirt, preferably made from three yards of fabric to ensure that it does not cling to the woman's legs. Over the buttoned up shirt is a vest. Stockings are worn, with the color varying from congregation to congregation. The very modest woman will wear two pairs of stockings. This may also stem from the fact that women are not allowed to shave their legs and wearing two pairs of stockings covers the leg hair.

The color of the attire plays almost as important a role as the clothing itself. No bright colors are allowed, especially shades of red. One former member recalls a time when she made her vest and skirt out of a dark burgundy fabric with small rust colored squares in it. Danny Layne stopped her and asked, "Why are you wearing a red polka dotted skirt?" She explained to him that the colors were burgundy and rust, assuring him that she would never wear red. "I said its red polka dot, so that's what it is," he replied. She didn't wear the outfit again.

The woman in the CoGR completes her outfit with a pair of black shoes with a less than two inch heel, but taller than those that would be considered flats. These are the clothes that are worn by women in all seasons. It is considered immodest to roll up one's sleeves even for washing the dishes, so the true Saint gets her sleeves wet.

On one visit I had with my children after the divorce, I took them to Paddock Lake in Kenosha County. The girls were dressed as is the CoGR tenet, with their long dresses and vests. They swam fully clothed, with their long skirts billowing up around them like a parachute. When my oldest son, who left the Cult with me, removed his shirt for swimming, my daughter Rachel immediately exited the water. She refused to be in the lake with anyone immodest, not even her own brother.

Another rule meant to keep a woman from being a temptress was that she must wear her hair in a bun at all times. No one should see her with her hair down, including the members of her family. A former member tells her experience with the rule about hair: "Danny said that we had to wash our hair and then immediately put it back up again, but one sister said that when she did that, her hair went moldy, so Danny said we were allowed to dry our hair with a hair dryer before we put it back into a bun. However, that it was not to be hanging down in front of our children and husbands... that would be immodest! "Another former member recalls that Danny Layne told her that wearing her hair down was considered "witchy" to the Saints.

For the men of the CoGR the rules concerning attire are similar. They wear only dark colors, their outfit consists of underwear, t-shirt, dark pants, a light colored, long sleeved, buttoned down shirt (buttoned to the top button) and a dark colored vest. Ties are not permitted. The pastors preached that only the fallen churches allow them. In keeping with the rules of modesty, men must always be fully clothed, and may not even shave without their buttoned shirt on in the men's bathroom at the camp meeting.

The O'Sheas brought a man named Booker from Chicago to a camp meeting in Ohio. He was caught shaving with only a t-shirt on. He was told not to do it again, he was only a visitor. When he was caught again he was kicked out of the campgrounds. He had nowhere to go, as he had ridden in with Pat O'Shea and his family.

Gold or anything gold colored was forbidden. This includes wedding bands. If a woman was to buy a purse or a pair of shoes with gold buckles, she must paint over the gold color with black nail polish.

I once had a confrontation with Pat O'Shea regarding the edict against gold. I asked O'Shea which scripture in the Bible condemns owning gold. He replied that the verse was Peter 3:3 "And do not let your adornment be that of the external (broiding -KJV) and of the putting on of gold adornments or the wearing of outer garments." I pointed out that the CoGR was being inconsistent in their teachings. The verse includes three areas of concern and not just one. The areas are 1.)not broiding your hair or 2.)of wearing of gold or 3.)wearing of outer garments. I told him if it means NO gold, then it must be consistent with NO clothes. He stated that the verse was telling us not to have "extra" clothing. I said this would mean we shouldn't have then only "extra" gold either, instead of NO gold. The last time I checked, Pat O'Shea was still wearing clothes. Braiding and broiding are two different things. Broiding is weaving things like strands of colorful decoration or gold into the hair. To be consistent with that scripture I believe the emphasis is applied to where the focus is. Don't focus or be consumed by decorating oneself with broiding, gold, or clothes. Where is one's heart's focus?

The baby's and children's standard of dress, will resemble the parents dress code. There is almost NO baby or children's clothes in the typical department stores that is appropriate enough to be "Saintly". Almost everything has to be made by the members themselves. The women would love to be notified of where they could buy a baby's dress that is dark colored, with long sleeves with the dress part going down to their ankles. Little girls must learn to crawl in a dress like that. I have seen little girl babies having to learn how to crawl like an animal on all fours with their knees up in the air. It is nearly impossible to crawl with the dress restricting or binding up around the knees. Also there is NO lace, monogram, or designs on their clothing. Absolutely NO cartoon character like Mickey Mouse will be found anywhere in the house, toy box, or on their clothing.

There is a long list of places the members cannot go. The list includes all amusement parks and even some museums. Danny Layne would even go to a military type of museum but doesn't allow viewing of any movies or videos to be done. He will say where members of the CoGR can take their families: to church, and get-together-s with other members, or camp meetings.

Church services can last for hours and everyone is expected to remain attentive throughout, including small children. If a child is to become restless and squirms or falls asleep during church services, parents have on hand small sticks for swatting the children. The CoGR has received much negative attention in regards to their views on child rearing.

The music during services is completely acappella, as no musical instruments are allowed in church. There are also no crosses or celebrations of holidays. In order to miss a service you must have prior approval from the pastor.

Camp meetings were tightly structured gatherings, with the entire day being scheduled from 7 in the morning until lights out at 11 pm. Prayer meeting in the morning was not an option if you want to attend or not. Everyone MUST attend including small children. It consists of one or two prayer related songs. Then one minister gets up and preaches a short message on prayer or about a Bible character that had a prayer life. Then for the remainder of the service everyone gets on their knees and several people pray.

After that, is breakfast and the dining room and outside areas fill up with conversation as they eat. The kitchen duties of cooking, cleaning, and washing dishes get rotated throughout the several days. There is a schedule list of which State or which age bracket has the duty for which days. The local congregation of where that particular meeting is held is responsible for the actual cooking or delegating of it and all the other jobs like cleaning bathrooms or shuttling people from the airport.

The morning service begins usually about 10:00 am and lasts at least two hours. Everyone must attend. After service is out there is a little bit of visiting. However, as far as I remember, by about 1:00 pm, there is a demanded quiet time for sleeping or reading.

If I remember correctly, about 2:00 pm, the dinner bell sounds and people head for the dining area. The meals are good and creative at keeping the cost down.

Shortly after that meal the several children age groups have their service. Middle age and older people can sit in on their groups or study and pray for the evening service.

The evening service, was about 7:00 pm, and lasted about two hours. If visitors came, this would be the service that they probably would attend.

The last meal immediately followed that service which was sometime after 9:00 pm. By about 10:00 pm most people are heading for their dorm or cabin. No noise is allowed after 11:00 pm.

One of the main unusual events for the yearly National camp

meeting held in West Melton, Ohio, is the street meetings held in Dayton, Ohio. The morning or actually noon service gets drastically shortened with just a few comments. Danny Layne instructs the congregation on what to do and what not to do. When the congregation of a few hundred people, arrive in downtown Dayton, they fill up a parking lot especially reserved for just this group. They will then have a long line of people all dressed in their normal attire which resembles the 1800's type of dress. There is a place in the heart of that city that is like a park with the tall buildings all around it. There is a stage that can be reserved by bands and things of that nature. Part of this congregation gets up on that stage and starts singing all their religious songs. While that is going on, some of the congregation stands back and watches the special singers as if they are the audience. Danny had instructed that it takes the uneasiness away from the general public if they can blend in the already established audience. In one of the first years, the group made the mistake of all standing in front as special singers which caused a shying away from the general public. Having nearly five hundred people stand in a group, facing you while they sang, all in their long dresses, would make you feel like you are being attacked by them.

So Danny realized that and ordered that most of the congregation should act like the audience to draw the public in closer in behind them. It worked and many office workers would come down from the tall buildings surrounding this plaza and take their lunch break amongst us. At the same time, a part of the congregation walked the surrounding blocks and passed out hundreds of gospel tracks. The unique thing about this type of evangelizing is that this cult put their best behavior and practices forward and hid the most offensive things. None of the parents are supposed to have any of their discipline sticks. All the evidence remotely exposing any of this was left in the vehicles. And the most peculiar thing that Danny ordered for us to refrain from, is not to practice our "Holy Kiss" when we are in this public setting. It would be offensive to the common person.

They have a doctrine of kissing. There is a scripture in the Bible that instructs us to greet each other with a Holy kiss. They take it out of context and add inconsistencies. Men only embrace and kiss men while women only embrace and kiss women. I remember Danny Layne making a big issue out of that doctrine and stated that he could detect the low spirituality of the ones that resist doing that. He mentioned that kissing on the lips is the proper place to kiss since there was a verse that stated to kiss the lips of them that bring good tidings.(Proverbs 24:26?)

A trademark of a cult is to pick and choose what they want to adhere to and what they will reject. They will humanly think away anything that they don't want which creates an inconsistency. Does the scripture differentiate between genders while making the point of Holy kissing? I don't think so. Instead of seeing that conduct as a custom, Danny Layne fights to keep that practice but adds to scripture by enforcing a gender separation, which is contrary to the open statement.

The reasoning behind his argument to enforce that doctrine could derive from his past. He had been a heavy heroine addict for about nineteen years. In order to support his drug addiction he became a homosexual prostitute. This teaching of his might have something to do with his prior behavior when he performed for several years. He must have done this, not out of a genuine love or emotion, but instead out of duty to compensate for his addiction. I surmise that all the modesty rules that he enforces, also were created to compensate for what he participated in years earlier.

I remember vividly how Danny demonstrated with his mouth, how to kiss properly another brother of the church. He displayed what he called a non-affectionate kiss. I can envision it as a method of action where pay is a factor to satisfy another's weakness or addiction. If one of their women preaches a "good" message, will Danny "kiss the lips of those that bring good tidings?" Or does he think, if it is a woman, that it is not good tidings? What if he preaches a message? Will the women of the congregation kiss him for bringing good tidings?

Church of God Restoration members are not to consume caffeine, or alcohol, even if in sauces or imitation vanilla, or fermented soy sauce. They are not permitted to patronize supper clubs or festivals in which alcohol is being served. There are some contradictions, as chocolate, which contains caffeine is not forbidden. Instead of Danny accepting chocolate as having caffeine, he permitted it by excusing it because it would take a truckload to receive a dose like he claimed coffee had. Is sin then OK if taken in tiny amounts?

Dating is forbidden. Marriages are arranged by the pastor.

Danny Layne once preached in front of just the congregation at a camp meeting when there were no visitors, at how we must deal with outsiders that are not part of our group. We do not tell everyone of what we do and don't believe in. That could make them unreachable for us to draw them into the fold. He mentioned how a neighbor gave him a Santa Claus coffee cup for Christmas. "I could have told her that we don't celebrate Christmas because it is a pagan holiday, or that Santa Claus is the form of anti-Christ, but instead we need to show gratitude and love toward them. It was a cup that she might have spent close to ten dollars on. Instead of telling her all of the evil things about the gift, I thanked her. I left the cup in view at first where she could see it, but then eventually moved it into the cupboard, way in the back. After a while I can throw it away," he told us.

There are jobs which CoGR members are not allowed to have. The list includes police officers, any jobs related to fixing or selling televisions, jobs in the medical field, stock broker, over the road trucker(when he has a family)lawyers, politicians, judges, or any job that would place a member in a forbidden place, such as a casino or supper club. A military position is ungodly. A man, whom I will call "Scott", had been in the military a long time. I think it was his nineteenth or his twentieth year when he met this cult. Within a few weeks the cult had convinced him that he needed to quit. Just months shy of retirement he gave it all up and refused all pay. He was placed before a psychologist or psychiatrist to evaluate if Scott had gone crazy. Just being cult-crazy didn't qualify.

Children are home schooled or sent to schools run by the

CoGR. College is discouraged.

The church preaches against pledging allegiance to the American flag, stating that the only allegiance members should have is to God and the CoGR. When the Kenosha, Wisconsin congregation under the ministry of Pat O'Shea, took a church property from some other people legally by deception, we were left with a building that had a large cross in the front of the sanctuary, along with an American flag. The flag was thrown away, and the cross was taken down and busted up so that it could fit in the dumpster also. Disrespect to the American flag continues.

This last summer, I believe it was July of 2007, I had all my children together for a full week placement. I took them to a lumberjack competition show in Stillwater, Minnesota. I remembered a new rule of this cult just before my wife left me that had not been mentioned when I first was attracted to this group. I later heard preaching which was against the American flag and how it is sinful to say the pledge or honor the flag.

Before the lumberjack competition began, the typical display of the flag and the anthem was sung. The entire crowd stood up out of respect. I looked toward my five children and they were defiantly sitting down. Randy and David, my two oldest boys which are in my placement, were standing and irritated also at the defiant show of disrespect. My oldest brainwashed daughter, Rachel, folded her arms and made sure that the other four children would NOT stand up. I knew that the four younger children would receive punishment when they got back home if they dared to violate the church/cult's teachings. It was humiliating to be next to such a defiant demonstration opposing the flag. Why does the cult though then want to partake of freedoms of this country (religion) when they despise it?

Members of the CoGR do not see doctors or seek medical attention, even in the most dire of circumstances. This teaching has caused the deaths of many members, including children. After receiving much backlash from the media, the CoGR released this statement in 2002:

WHEREAS: Our national, state/provincial and local

governments have passed laws with severe penalties, limiting our liberty to treat our seriously ill minor children exclusively with spiritual means.

RESOLVED; Having the best interest of our children in mind, in cases of perceived serious illness of one of our minor children, the ministry shall advise the parents/guardians of their legal requirement and allow seeking of medical means for the child according to the law of the land.

This statement amounts to little more than just the CoGR trying to cover their tracks. The reality is that any member who seeks medical attention for themselves or their children will be viewed as spiritually weak.

I was called into Pat O'Shea's office to be reprimanded on what would become just one of many occasions. On this occasion, I had purchased an inhaler for my asthmatic son. I was tired of sitting back and watching my son struggle for air, with or without their prayers. They preached divine healing, but at no point during my time with the CoGR had I ever seen it work.

"People die in hospitals, too," Pat said to me once in the midst of an argument.

"If ten people walked in the hospital with a ruptured appendix, all ten would probably walk out," I said. "On the other hand, if they were in only this church's care, I would hope that maybe one would live!"

I purchased a set of colored index cards. I used a different color for each of the four Gospels. I wrote on the cards the miracles Jesus performed from each of the Gospels. Each healing miracle was placed on a separate card. It was amazing how each time the word "immediately" or words like that were used each time the miracle was performed. The common thread I found throughout was that each of the healings was performed with instant results, unlike the CoGR, who would pray for days hoping for a positive outcome.

I presented my project to Pat O'Shea the pastor of the Kenosha, Wisconsin congregation. I instructed him to make two piles by separating the instantaneous healings from the ones that took time.

It only took about the first ten cards for him to see the pattern of all of them going on the one instantaneous pile. He quit and gave me the cards back. His attitude changed and he ridiculed me for questioning church doctrine. For me to do that, meant that I had a serious demented spiritual condition. I must seek God and repent. I should at least stand up before the congregation and apologize for my lack of faith and have them pray for me to get some understanding.

CHAPTER 4
<u>CHILD ABUSE</u>

Even though the cult did not believe in medicine or doctors, I found it ironic of all their contradictions. I disputed that the members still used eye doctors and dentists. I was soon informed that with dentists, all the pulling of teeth or root canals was done without any anesthesia like novocaine.

During my time with the CoGR I saw many children beaten until they were bruised black and blue. They taught that the punishment was to continue until the child had submitted completely. This meant the prescribed number of swats did not begin until the child laid, by his own accord, still and quiet until the spanking ended. Because of this extreme barbaric procedure a child often would acquire black and blue marks. Sue, the pastor's wife used to be a nurse before she became part of this cult. She would instruct parents that if they beat their children (disciplined according to their speech), and the child would receive bruises that they were supposed to soak the child in Epsom Salt. Is that not medical attention?

Parents in the CoGR were given a copy of the 1999 publication "Mommy, Daddy, We Would See Jesus!", as a child-rearing handbook, written by a pastor's wife Theresa Storts. While promoting a loving relationship between parent and child, the author also endorses spanking a child, as young as six months with an appropriately sized wooden dowel. "The size of the dowel should vary with the age of the child ...the smallest 1/8 inch diameter dowel rod.... is fine for a child two years old and younger."

I sat behind the pastor's wife, Sue, for several years and witnessed her cruelty that she inflicted on her children. If one of her two, three, or four year olds was not sitting still in church service or falling asleep, she would take the dowel and strike it across the back of the child's hand. If that created excessive crying the child would be rushed to the back of the church or to the basement to get a much greater beating. It was easy to hear the echoes of that beating inside the sanctuary even if she was downstairs. Several times my wife diaper changed one of their children and told me as a discipline form that we were not out of line, that their children were black and blue also.

I despised their teaching on how to discipline properly. Danny stated that even just a few months old baby can be trained to take their nap without fussing. One swat and a forceful voice to go "Night, Night", is a good start. The baby can be trained very quickly if you are forceful.

I witnessed Danny Layne demonstrate this curbing at an Ohio camp meeting one time. The service had just begun and it was now time for the message by one of the ministers. Everyone waited in silence as if God was about to do a miracle. Suddenly a pastor from California stands up and heads for the pulpit. Many "Amens" broke the silence since God once again displayed his power by providing us a message bearer.

This pastor's young boy was left unattended on the front pew. The pulpit is on an elevated platform with several pews on the side of it for the prominent people. Danny Layne sits on the closest pew facing the pulpit. He got the attention of the child on the first pew of the general congregation and motioned for him to be quiet. The boy's father began preaching. Soon the boy started to wiggle and squirm again. Danny Layne had warned him once and it was show down time now. Danny got off of his lofty place, walked down to this boy, picked him up, and walked down the aisle to the back of the church. I was in the back and just outside of the building holding one of my fussy babies. Once Danny stepped out of the building he made a right turn and headed for the kitchen and dining building. While he was heading that way he picked up a stick from the ground. He disappeared in the building for quite a while.

After a while he was returning holding this teary eyed boy that was trying to stifle his crying. Before they went past me, Danny once more motioned for the boy to quit this gasping and stifling of the sobbing, and just quit! With that done he carried him back up front and this little black boy sat quietly beside this old pastor that is white. The boy and his family were black. The reason I mention color is to make the point that it was not the parent or even a relative that did the disciplining.

The cult taught that the parent must break the will of the child. If they don't break the child's strong will when they are young, the child will be of no use later. When a child breaks or violates a rule, there is a discipline that the child must willfully submit to. They must on their own bend over the bed, chair or sofa to receive their designated swats. Any wrestling and swatting prior to that is extra punishment to break their will and is not part of the punishment for their violation.

Stevie's Abuse

My family was at the Ohio camp meeting and the morning service had just begun. My family could nearly fill up a pew all by ourselves. Within the first song or two, I noticed my wife and my five year old Stevie were missing. I did not notice them leave so I turned around to see if I could locate them. I did not see them anywhere so I just continued singing. In about fifteen minutes Shereen returned by herself and sat down by me. She mentioned that she needed my help in giving Steve a spanking. I asked what he did and she said that he stuck out his tongue, not at her, but just stuck it out when she told him to sit still. "Have you spanked him some?", I asked, knowing that this might be this cults issue of submitting which is the problem. "You know what the church teaches!" was her forceful response. Oops, I am dealing with someone that is upset and I must be careful or my marriage will be broke up and I will be driving back to Wisconsin by myself.

"Did you spank him some?" I ask. "You know what the church teaches!" she responded. "If you don't help me I will go to the ministry!"

This is going to be tough. If I don't help her, my family will be taken from me and I will go back to Wisconsin without them until I submit to all the church teachings. If I do go to the cabin I must battle against my conscience in dealing with this cruelty. What can I do? I followed her to our cabin. In this cabin I saw this pathetic little boy that looked like he already received enough discipline. Fear was written all over him. I wished it was me instead of him but I too would not be able to lie across the bed without being held there.

I start pleading with him to submit to the church's teachings. Counting to ten or whatever other techniques do not help. Shereen insists that I must hold him so that she can spank. As soon as I grab Steve, he begins to scream. I immediately cup my hand over his mouth with one hand, while I restrain him across my lap with my other hand. Using one of my legs to pin his legs across my other leg, I provided his bottom to his mother that demanded this procedure. She beat the stick on his rear about twenty or thirty times. I was allowed to release him hoping that this was the end of it. Once again she demanded him to lay across the bed. He could not, and so the discipline had not yet begun!

I was forced to wrestle with him again, and he received another twenty or thirty swats with the stick. Release again and he still could not submit. Over and over again with this same wrestling and beating. He must have received somewhere between three to five hundred swats before we broke his stubborn will according to the cult. This beating lasted about two hours because the long church service was already out when he finally yielded. As soon as he bent over the bed on his own I glared at my wife to softly just tap him for his designated five swats for his violation. I am glad that she obeyed me at least on that.

The next day Shereen ordered me to give Steve and Joel the four year old brother their shower. What a horror to my eyes which I will never forget! Upon undressing him for his shower I saw a mass of black, blue, purple, green, red, yellow and every other color of the rainbow, covering my poor Stevie's bottom from his belt area down to his back of his knee area. I felt like crying. Never have I ever seen such bruising in my life.

"Steve, what happened?"

He hung his head sheepishly, and said that he got a spanking.

I asked him, "Why?"

"Because I stuck my tongue out?"

"NO! That is not why you got that much spanking. Why did you get that?"

He looked confused. "Because I am five?"

Mercy! That is a sick humor. It is not because he is five. He does not even understand why. I had to explain to him about this cult teaching about submitting. Inside of me I purposed right there that I will never do this again. I might lose my family if I don't help abusing my children but I must appease my conscience. Different people asked me why I didn't go to authorities. When was I supposed to? Before or after this torture? If before, then there is no evidence and I would lose my family. And then, if after the event, even though she did all the hitting, I would be just as guilty for holding him. Even though I did not want to abide by the cult rules, I still became guilty of the same. I was blackmailed into it. When was I supposed to tell authorities? There are cases like that still in that cult.

Susy's Abuse

On many occasions I came home from work to find that one of the children was missing.

"Where is Suzy?" I would ask.

"She is waiting for you in the bathroom, " Shereen would answer.

In the bathroom I would inquire as to what had happened.

"Did you submit and lay across the toilet?" I asked Suzy.

"No," she said.

"Did mommy hit you?"

"Yes." Shereen had hit her randomly while Suzy tried to hide behind the toilet.

"What did you do wrong?"

"I wouldn't eat my lunch."

"You've been in here ever since?"

"Yes." The child had been sitting in the bathroom since noon and I had come home from work at six or seven o'clock.

I told her to holler while I softly gave her the required "spanking." I felt that sitting in the bathroom half the day was punishment enough, but knew that Shereen would not be satisfied unless the CoGR teachings had been fulfilled. She heard the fake crying and told the pastor. My days were numbered when he kept hearing how I didn't back my wife up that was trying to enforce the cult rules.

More Abuse

On one occasion I was awakened from sleep by the sounds of my children screaming and crying. I went to the children's rooms and found Shereen grabbing the children, one after the other, and spanking them in a fury. They ran around the beds trying to avoid her blows. I stood helpless, fearing that if I intervened, it would become more fuel added to the fire that Pat O'Shea had already set to my marriage. He would break my marriage up. When it was over I was able to discern that the children hadn't gone to bed after putting on their pajamas. They waited upstairs for her to read a bedtime story as she often did. When she didn't come they began to play. When Shereen caught them playing, she became angry and began striking them.

I have seen Shereen use wooden hair brushes, clothes hangers, shoes, wooden spoons or anything to inflict pain. I have witnessed her hitting the children in the head on occasions with instruments.

Beat by the Pastor

Shortly after we moved to Kenosha, I noticed several issues that I couldn't agree with. I addressed those issues since it was not my style to remain quiet. Because of that I was in the spotlight of the cult and the pastors. My pastor, Pat O'Shea, already hinted that he could tear my marriage apart, by saying that Shereen would have to look out for her own spiritual safety.

Home schooling had already been taken out of my hands. The cult was running an illegal private school. Sue O'Shea, the pastor's wife, was teaching the older children of this congregation, while Shereen was teaching the younger children. That is not legal according to the rules of Wisconsin. For the home schooling each year we would receive an application for the privilege of educating our children ourselves. There is a sentence on that application that basically states that home schooling must be done by the parents, or by a delegated close relative. Also, the criteria for home schooling, requires that it consists of only one family per unit. The church combines all families together, which becomes a private school.

My older children were therefore taught by Sue O'Shea. The issue of discipline came up and since I was in the spotlight of infuriating the paster by my other issues, I decided to permit the cult to discipline my children if absolutely necessary. I never dreamed of what liberty that allows.

I knew some of my children had been disciplined by Pat and Sue O'Shea but I did not understand what took place. It was not until after Shereen left me that I asked my oldest two boys what happened. They started exposing the beating the pastor and his wife did to them. Since Pat was a shop teacher at a public school in Illinois, he designed an instrument that was used for what they call discipline. The paddle was approximately sixteen inches long and about six inches wide. It was about an inch thick and resembled a breadboard with a handle.

After my wife left me, my oldest two boys had been working

with me that day and therefore, chose to stay with me instead of being under the influence of the cult. The day she left me she moved with my other five children right into the pastor's house. She was now in the same house as the man whom she admired and obeyed more than she did me. During the last couple of years she did whatever he asked her to do regardless if it was in contradiction to what I asked of her. My oldest two refused to go with her under those conditions of being forced to live with the people that whipped them. They had an animosity toward those two people that their mother was cleaving to so much.

So I inquired of them what had happened with the disciplining that had gone on in this illegal private school. They mentioned that both Pat and Sue had beat them with that paddle. They were required to bend over and grab their ankles and remain there until either of them quits hitting them. It not only was embarrassing, but they also stated that they received from them the most painful and forceful beating they ever got. It is still humiliating to think of it and especially when their Dad is writing a book telling the whole world about it.

One day while at the cult's illegal private school, the pastor's oldest son got in trouble for cutting up in class. His mother, Sue O'Shea, called him up front of the class and tried punishing him. He was in his senior year and not in position to be humiliated in front of the other students. So instead he tried making a joke out of it. Every time Sue would strike him with that paddle he would talk out loud and say, "Ouch Mommy, that hurts, Mommy!" That made my oldest son lose his composure and he accidentally laughed. That agitated Sue and she called him up front.

"Put your hands on the chalkboard and keep them there until I am finished", she demanded.
I never gave permission for something that stupid. No wonder my boys don't like her. When I was in the court battles, this abuse issue came up regarding what both Pat and Sue O'Shea had done to them. The Kenosha's legal system, both the courts and the law enforcement, looked into it but dismissed it for two reasons. One was because O'Sheas made it seem like it was many years ago. It

had only been thirteen months since the last abuse had happened. However, it was dismissed because there was a year statute of limitation for that is what I was told. About four years later I found out from an attorney (NOT from a Kenosha attorney) that said "No!, there is a three year limitation for that kind of crime". Either way, we were too late again.

The second reason my case was dismissed is that I gave them permission to discipline. I 'm sorry, but I did not think a bone breaking device was considered discipline. To me that is abuse. What could they use next and still call it discipline, a meat cleaver? Also I would never have given permission to beat a child for not holding their composure at something comical.

I brought this up to my last Judge Bruce E. Schroeder, about the abuse that was going on in the cult and how my boys were beat by the pastor and his wife. He said, "Hold it! I am not interested in hearing all that. I went to school too, and I got in trouble also. The principle did not use the paddles you are mentioning, but he used sawed-off golf clubs, and he pounded the dust out of my pants if you know what I mean." Most of the people in the back private chambers of the court room laughed. "But you know something about that? None of the students that got that type of beating from him had any lasting effect. So don't give me this about child abuse, I don't want to hear it and I don't care!"

Before he began this back room hearing he said everything would be off record. Therefore, no transcripts were documented of what was said. I desire that the judge, the court reporter, the secretary, the GAL, Shereen, her attorney, and myself, would all be separated and each placed in front of the lie detector machine, to evaluate who is telling the truth about if I am making up this stuff. What I just mentioned was said and it is true.

After I placed this story on my website, he really became angry with me. I didn't gain anything from him anymore and soon he asked me to ask him to recuse himself from my case. So I did ask, and he did recuse, making him the fifth judge that did not want my case and recused himself. I am not fighting a spouse for the right to remove my children from this wicked and abusive cult. I am fighting the courts and the cult themselves, and believe there is a money trail from them to the judges somehow.

After two years into my divorce, someone else started the website, www.screwedkenoshastyle.com for me. I desire for you to visit that site to get a greater understanding of what I have gone through. On it you will find pictures, newspaper articles, videos, tape recordings from the cult's church service and such, which could not be in this book because of legal issues like permissions from the cult, which would be impossible to get. I am grateful to the Internet that does not need permission. It just can't be a lie and therefore slanderous. This entire book and website is the truth.

Also while this book goes to print, I will be working on my second book, "Fighting the Black Robe Conspiracy". Hopefully I can get it published within two months after this book. That book will be more on my experiences with the justice system that so far has embraced this cult as the best place for my children to be in. If anything in this book stirs you and you would like to help me in this battle, please purchase this book and tell other people of this book. Tell your congregation about this to protect them from this cult and also to help me if they purchase this book. I was quoted by several good attorneys that to beat my case would require a deposit of about twenty thousand dollars. My goal and desire is to sell about twenty thousand books so I could hire that type of attorney. I want to thank you for your help.

Ohio Visit

My family was still living up in Northern Wisconsin when we decided to take a trip as a family to the Ohio/Indiana congregation of this cult. This was the first and only time we were in that area which was not when they had their large camp meeting. We wanted to be just amongst a congregation of that size to see what it was like. The adults could somewhat "hide" in a larger group like that. The children on the other hand had no escape and were forbidden to hide.

The service started with a age segregated Sunday school. The adults stayed in the main sanctuary while the children went downstairs. Before the hour was over the children came back upstairs and were brought in front of the adults. As a group they sang a couple of songs for us. Then the children one by one had to recite their memory verse for the week.

One older child recited his few verses with ease. Another child was scared and was having trouble in keeping from crying. His mother stood in front of him with a stick. "Don't look at them. Look at me. Now say your verse." The child is about three years old. Say, "God", the mother said to the child. The child's lips quivered but he managed to say, "God". The Mother continues by telling him to say, "is". The little child started to cry but once again the word "is" could barely be heard. The finishing word for that verse is, "love", but the child emotionally falls apart. The mother swats him with the stick right in front of everyone and tells him to stop. The strike of the stick only worsened the situation. The mother picks him up and heads for the back room of this building.

The next child in line stumbles through their recital as crying and the sounds of a beating is taking place in the back room. The next girl trembles in fear as she voices out what she had memorized. Her mother holding a stick in front of her provoked her to finish her requirement without breaking into uncontrollable crying. The boy that just got his whipping was placed back in front of us. This time, even though he was mildly crying, he could verbalize those three words, "God is love", while the mother held the stick in front of him. He survived this week but in just seven days he must face this same trauma again. Next week he must get the love of Jesus beat into him again, or at least until he can recite that "God is love".

Because we were visitors, my children were not required to stand up front and get whipped if they couldn't perform. Several children did receive the force of the stick that day. What I fear presently is that my younger children are now in that very same congregation. The courts have decided that my children are best off being with their mother who has them involved in this cult.

CHAPTER 5

MEDICAL NEGLECT

Sam

Whenever someone left this cult I try to hide their identity. The name is changed but the incidents are true and did happen. I was helping a pastor with some carpentry, (whom I will call Sam) formerly of this cult. "Sam" was building a garage for himself. Another church member was also helping whom I will call Mike.

We were working with nail guns which operate a lot like a gun with only one extra safety feature. There is a trigger on it which when compressed releases a plunger by compressed air which drives a 16d nail down "the barrel" and into the lumber instantly. With a pull of a trigger and a bang, the wood is secured with the nail sunk to its head.

The nails come in a coil rolled up with two rows of thin wire melted to each nail to secure them in place. When the nail gets "shot" the two wires break, taking only the two pieces of wire along which is directly attached to that nail.

The safety feature is at the end of the "barrel", where the nail comes out. It is a bracket that sticks out slightly longer than the barrel. It is rigged on a spring that can slide up the barrel so that the barrel must touch the wood. If the barrel is not touching the wood, you can pull the trigger all you want, but it does not shoot any nails. A person could take one hand and slide the bracket up the barrel, and then pull the trigger with the other hand. With that technique a person could shoot nails at objects over fifty yards away.

We were putting on the outside board onto the gable end of the roof. While Mike and I were holding the middle and bottom end of the board, Sam was trying to nail the peak. He was lying down on the roof reaching over the edge of the roof in an awkward position. From that strange position he realized that he could not nail with his superior right hand. So he switched the nail gun into his left hand. Holding the board in place now with his right hand he proceeded to shoot a nail with the nail gun which was in his left hand. The shot was good except that the gun bounced and landed the second time directly right on Sam's right hand. Because of his inferior capability hand which had less dexterity and control he shot and nearly buried a nail into his right hand. Less than a quarter inch was sticking out in the meaty part at the base of his thumb. Instantly he dropped the nail gun and said "Praise the Lord".

The cult was taught that whatever happens in life, that your response should always be "Praise the Lord". You have a car accident, or your house just burned down, or your legs just got blown off by a terrorist, your commanded response is supposed to be, "Praise the Lord!"

Sam then said that he shot himself, loud enough for the families in the house to hear it. We came off the roof and evaluated the situation. Sam tried pulling the nail himself but it would not budge. You would think a smooth nail would just slide back out when in flesh, but something was wrong here.

Now we have a predicament. Sam is a preacher of this cult that does not believe in doctors or medicine. What do we do now? Well, the decision was made to go to the hospital just to get the nail pulled out. All surgery or medication will be rejected, just get the nail out!

With Sam in the passenger seat, his wife in the back seat, and I behind the wheel, we left in a hurry to the hospital. It felt strange to intentionally violate the speed limit, not reckless but yet way over legal limit.

The doctor ordered immediately some x-rays to see what he was up against. Sam complied and soon we saw what was the difficulty. I had walked out of Sam's room down the hall and past the x-ray evaluation room. There was no door and I saw two nurses and the doctor studying the x-ray picture. It was strange to see the transparent picture of the flesh and bones of a hand revealed, but then with a black foreign object almost buried completely through the hand almost coming out in the meaty area opposite from the thumb.

The doctor did not see me behind him so he felt the liberty to be a comedian to the nurses. He started shaking his hands as if he was shivering from hypothermia or fear, and said that he will have to pull that nail out now. It was funny but he said, oops – sorry, when he turned around and spotted me. I smiled and asked him about some of the details of that photo. The nail had missed all the bones and main arteries. However, the little wires that break off with each nail were acting like a fishhook. The flesh will have to rip to get it out!

The doctor told Sam that he will need to get Novocaine shots into his hand to numb the pain. At that Sam said that he will not allow that because of religious convictions. That marveled the doctor and stunned him a little bit. He mentioned the wire barbs and that it would be painful and if he chose at any time to change his mind, it would be OK.

So with the locking pliers in hand, the tug-of-war began. I was asked to help pull Sam's hand the opposite direction that the doctor and his plier were pulling. I am sure I was pulling a hundred pounds of force. I saw the nail move a little and the flesh bulging around the area. Without any pain killer the doctor had to cut some of the flesh to release the wire barbs. Watching a little more of this pulling and cutting and I started feeling myself getting sick. Things started to spin and I excused myself and reclined in the chair nearby. That is when everyone noticed how white I was and suddenly attention was diverted from Sam to me. No, take care of him. I will be fine if I can divert my attention away to something totally different than this barbaric procedure.

After the episode was over, I started contemplating over what happened. X-rays are basically radiation. As chemotherapy, radiation consists of harmful rays that last in the body possibly months or years. Pregnant women are not supposed to have any. Restrictions are made on how many a person can have over a certain period of time. Lead aprons are used to control the rays from other parts of the body. The x-ray technician that takes them steps out of the room for each shot. They do have consequences that have a prolonged duration of risk.

That made me consider the inconsistency of the teaching of this cult. First the cult likes using the verse in James 5:14 where it mentions what the church is supposed to do with sick people. They add to the scripture by including everyone that got injured. They also add to it by rejecting every method contrary to prayer. And yet they do a lot of things besides just prayer when THEY choose to.

If someone fell through the ice on a lake and suffered hypothermia I am sure they would do more than pray. They would get them out of the wet freezing clothes, into a warm or hot bath. They would get them into warm and dry clothes. All of these things are not mentioned in that verse. Ironic though is that they teach that if doctor or medicine is not mentioned in that verse then God is not pleased with us when we use them.

Now the thing that I could not comprehend is the inconsistency with the two forms of "medicine" in my "Sam" story. Novocaine is a drug that enters into a body and leaves it within a few hours or possibly a day. That is wrong to use by the cult and supposedly displeases God. However, they believed an x-ray is only a picture and therefore not wrong. I could not comprehend how radiation was permitted while a simple drug was rejected. Where is the sensibility in that?

Another inconsistency is when Sue O'Shea the pastor's wife, encourages parents to soak their children in Epsom salt if their discipline teachings leave black and blue marks. "If you bruise your children by disciplining the way we teach, soak them in Epsom Salt!"

C-Section

Members of the cult have faced death by practicing this strange conviction. Expectant mothers and unborn babies have died because of it. If there is prolonged labor of a birth which has complications, death will usually be the result. "Still born" could be the cover up explanation of a child's death, if it died because of a too lengthy time for labor.

Rhoda was one of those skeletons in the cult's closet. She was the mother that was in labor for days, so I was told. She died exhausted but brought a child into the world moments before she left it.

Susan M. is one of the cult's main pastors. She is also the editor for their Gospel Trumpet paper. One thing that was kept a secret from most of the common members of the cult at the time was a medical incident that most did not know about. Susan had been pregnant and went into labor. I heard that she had been in labor for a few days and growing weak. It appeared that she was going to die.

Her husband, and her pastor who is no longer with this cult, made the radical decision to rush her to the hospital. A quick c-section was required which saved her life barely, but it was too late for the baby. The blame for the medical intervention was placed on the pastor and her own husband. The incident was covered up amongst the members. I had found out about it from my wife who said I wasn't supposed to tell it to anyone. The pastor, and Susan's husband, were considered to be "Unsaved" for doing that and that it was all their fault. They would be required to repent for that.

Why was Susan excused from being guilty partially herself? A pastor or minister in that cult that "sins" according to what they call a sin gets removed from their position without ever getting restored. Susan M. is one of their most important leaders and also the chief editor for their paper and difficult to replace.

Therefore, the rumor was started that when she went to the hospital and received this major surgery with medication and all, that she was pretty much out of it. Now if she was that far out of it, why was she capable of signing her own admittance? I heard that she was the one that signed her name so that they could treat her.

Death of Baby

In Kenosha Wisconsin, our local group (shortly before I considered them to have the trademarks of a cult), was trying to organize a large meeting. At the time we gathered in a small store front that could only seat about fifty people, or maybe a hundred packed very tight. The pastor, Pat, announced that we would need to find a much larger building to rent for the meeting and told us to keep our eyes open for opportunities.

The assistant pastor, who is no longer part of this group, mentioned that there was a church building on 75th street that we could probably rent. He offered to check into it. He found out that there was hardly anybody attending it, because most members were attending other churches even though they were members here. He also found out that the only requirement to be a member of that church is to be there for six consecutive weeks. What happened after that materialized into us being the majority, which resulted in us controlling it. Once we were the power we (the ministry of us), ran to an attorney and gave our property away to the Church of God trust fund. At that moment all the former members which were absent lost their building. They were not there so they didn't hear about the scheduled meeting about the vote to give the property. We legally took it from them for the approximate mortgage balance remaining at about $20,000.! For the new price of a good car, we swindled a property that was worth almost a half a million dollars. I heard they eventually sold it for about $300,000.

We organized a full week of services in this place with both weekends included. The main king-pin, the master-mind and founder of this cult, Danny Layne, was going to be the main speaker. When he is not giving a special meeting to one of the congregations, he resides in California. Saturday and Sunday went by uneventful but Monday something had gone wrong. Danny got up in front of the congregation about a half hour before the service began and announced an urgent need. He started out by addressing us with, "Saints, we need to get a hold of God!" They refer themselves as the "Saints", all other people are the Aint's.

So we as the Saints get informed about a need back in California that is just happening. The Wieb's baby is very sick! We need to get a hold of God. The congregation got down on their knees and several people prayed. However the next day, Danny got up but with a lot more urgency. He clapped his hands together and said that Wieb's need our prayers because the child is very sick and weak. We need to get a hold of God. If we do not get a hold of God the child could even die. They knew the seriousness of the child's condition. He continued by saying that he does not want to hear one person pray at a time. If every person in the world prayed, God could hear and separate each and every prayer. He is asking for all of us to pray at once. The place got pretty loud inside. That was the only medical attention the child received.

Wednesday and Thursday were a lot quieter with just a casual, "Remember the Wieb's" mentioned. Friday was awfully quiet so I approached Danny and asked him how Wieb's baby was doing. He hung his head, remained quiet about five seconds, and then responded that it had died. The baby died being only eleven months old because of this cult's doctrines. I often wondered at why they followed a doctrine where they have failed, I believe, every time. I don't ever remember seeing an instantaneous healing. Could God be possibly turning his ear and sight away from these people that have such arrogant, self-righteous attitudes about themselves? Or could God be angry with their deceptive lies and actions like the statement made in the courtroom?

The death of the child caused the parents to go in and out of the jail and courtrooms. In the courtroom the question was asked of why they did not seek medical attention? The real answer would rest in their religious teaching placed upon them by the cult.

However, the answer given was that, "we didn't know how sick the child was". On the surface it sounds OK, but knowing the below surface story of "the child could even die!" (as Danny told the congregation), was in contradiction to their response. Did they lie then? This is where I want to reveal their "loaded language" or speech they use. Nobody knows exactly when we will die or how sick we are. We might be loaded with cancer this very moment and about to die. The baby might seem about to die but still we really don't know for sure.

Ralph

To persuade me to move with my family to Kenosha Wisconsin, the cult provided us the upstairs of the assistant pastor's large house. It was located right next door to the pastor's house. My family had to share the downstairs kitchen with the rest of the household. An old man, Ralph Salz, was also living downstairs in this house. I remember him talking about wanting to go back to Missouri to visit his daughters and other family members.

That desire was heard by the pastor, Patrick O'Shea. He disapproved of Ralph even considering a trip like that. All church members must get approval from their pastor before they can do any major decision or any activity like that. They also must get approval, to see their relatives, or to buy a car, or what kind of car, or even to buy a major kitchen appliance.

I remember Ralph's troubled demeanor when Pat disallowed his desire of travel to see his daughters. That stirred my mind a little in contemplation about what kind of dictatorship that this might be, where a forty-five year old pastor can prevent an over eighty year old man from visiting his family?

I watched with interest as I saw a somewhat secret skirmish taking place between Ralph and this controlling minister. Because he was bucking the ministry he was questioned about the integrity of his salvation. Another doubt of that arose because Ralph would wear clothes that were not "Saintly" according to the church. He preferred wearing shirts, pants, and suits that had stripes or a design in the fabric. That was a contentious issue for the minister.

One day while I was away with my family, Ralph had a stroke. It appeared that he tried opening a window and just collapsed behind the sofa. The assistant pastor's son found him later like that when he entered the house. Ralph was carried into his bed and cared for by the church members. No medicine or doctors were ever provided for him. He may have received something to eat during the next two weeks, but I never witnessed it. All I remember is his constant cry for water. The nearly constant cry of "Water, water" is still haunting my memory. The simple cure of IV's was medical intervention and therefore condemned by this cult. Even a spoonful of water provoked him to vomit it back up.

It was about two weeks later that my wife and I received a knock on our bedroom door in the middle of the night. We were told that Brother Ralph Salz had just passed away. After hurriedly getting dressed we went downstairs to view the dead body. Pat O'Shea had been at Ralph's bedside that night when he died. Pat explained to us the details. His breathing had been restless and irregular that evening. Suddenly he had taken several short breaths and then one long breath. After a little pause he exhaled without taking another breath. Within a minute or two Pat knew that Ralph had passed away.

Now within ten minutes after he died, we stood around his bedside witnessing an experience that I will never forget. After Pat and his wife Sue, his oldest two or three children, the assistant's pastor's son, and my wife and I were there, Pat made a phone call. He called the master mind, Danny Layne in California. The assistant pastor was at his third shift job and could not come home.

"Praise the Lord" was the conversation on the phone. "Yes, Amen!" is the standard response which is a rule or requirement in this cult.
Pat announces that, "Brother Salz just passed away!

I was standing right there and witnessed everything. Listening to the one side of a phone conversation a person can piece together what both sides are saying.

"No, we can not call for help now since CPR would be automatically performed. We can't allow that to happen."

"Whatever you do, don't ever call the police for something like this; you must dial 911".

The cult and Danny Layne had experienced throughout several years on what works and what does not when dealing with the law and this freedom of religion. If you call the cops you are admitting that you are guilty. If you call 911, it releases you from fault. The only issue that needs to be addressed at this point is that the body must be positively dead before calling for emergency help. The pastors hung up the phone and we deliberately waited. I will never forget how we waited about an hour for the body to cool down and then what happened at that next phone call.

Pat was sitting beside the bed with one hand on the dead man's forehead, and in his other hand the phone calling Danny Layne the Master Mind.

"Praise the Lord" says the voice on the other end.

"Yes, Amen. The body is cool to the touch!" responds Pat O'Shea.

"Good. Now you can call 911. However, are not Brother Bernie's children in this house?" asks Danny

"Yes", responds Pat.

"Take them over to your house. This house is going to be filled up with a lot of people. We don't need to draw attention to ourselves like that. The authorities might ask questions and possibly ask the children which would not be good. Once you have them removed from that house you can then call 911. I marveled at how it was planned even though the corpse had been dead now for over an hour.

Just like Danny Layne had said, the house filled up with policemen, firemen, and even a mortician. Most of them rushed into the bedroom while the church members stayed in the living room. The flashes from the camera taking pictures reflected into the living room. Then in just a short time a higher officer confronted Pat O'Shea right there in the living room as I was a witness standing beside him.

"It appears that the body has been dead quite a while already. Why did you not call 911 any sooner?" asked this police officer.

My insides turned into a knot. I had listened to Pat O'Shea preach a message against me about truthfulness. He mentioned that if someone asks you a question and you know what they are talking about, answer it correctly. He said if the pastor asks a question don't hide the truth with evasive answers. He should not need to ask you the same question several different ways, to get to the bottom of what he wants to know. If you are answering it in a way that might not be a lie, but still not the answer you know that he is looking for, that is Deception. And deception is brother to a lie, and a lie makes you a liar, and a liar goes to hell!

How is Pat going to answer this question now? The honest answer according to his sermon is to say that we deliberately waited so that CPR could not be done because of religious reasons. Instead I was amazed at how Pat violated his own sermon that he preached against me, because I had been evasive toward him. I didn't like him needing to know every detail of my life so that he could control me more.

Now he was failing the test of honesty as I watched. He started by going into great detail at how Ralph had acted that night, at his irregular breathing and so forth. All the details at how he took his last breath and how he waited for another one, was elaborated on. Then, the details of how the church (us), gathered together first which needed to get dressed and such things like that. We had to then decide on what is the proper thing to do in a case like this. After much talking Pat finished the conversation by saying that because of all of these things, a little time must have slipped by. Wow! What a lie! A lie of omission at its finest coming from my pastor! I had a strong gut feeling that I made a mistake moving down to Kenosha. However, I was caught in the trap because Shereen was not going to leave Kenosha now. If she was told to choose between this cult and me, she already had told me before, "Well, I am not leaving here!" What amazes me is how this cult has enough faith to just let somebody die, but then doesn't have enough faith to tell the truth to the authorities. Is not obedience of telling the truth before God better than sacrifice?

After a couple days I noticed a change in Pat O'Shea's attitude toward the deceased. Before his death Ralph was always harped upon as being somebody that was bucking against this One, True Church and its doctrines. He was always considered in great danger of not making heaven if he did not get some strong spiritual help. That attitude all changed by our next church service. Pat preached and praised Brother Salz as if he was the greatest evangelist that had ever lived. "Oh, he was a good brother in the Lord" I would hear Pat say often.

It had been several months or maybe even years prior to Ralph's death that Pat was placed as a guardian or co-owner of Ralph's bank accounts and also of his car. Immediately after his death Patrick started driving Ralph's car constantly until it finally broke down and then eventually discarded. I don't know how much his bank accounts were either, but one thing I feel that happened is that there was enough money there to cloud the thinking capacity of Pat. From the pulpit he would preach what a good "brother" he had been and then gave him credit for what other ministers had said. Ralph had listened to a sermon from the preacher whom I already mentioned that had his son beaten by Danny Layne at the Ohio meeting. What that pastor had preached on one of the recordings, Ralph narrated to Pat. Later when Pat preached about Ralph, he mentioned that he had such great insight and repeated what was shared. Ralph got the credit for what the other pastor had preached.

Gerald T.

I knew this young man from the mid-1990's when I first met this group. He impressed me as being not overbearing even after he became pastor in his mid- twenties. I could easily approach him with issues that were troubling me. Never would he accuse me of being in great spiritual danger if I questioned certain tough points of this church that I had issues with. Pat was not that way toward me. In contrast to Pat, I felt challenged but yet relaxed with Gerry.

It was after my family had already been ripped from me when this incident happened. Gerry was working high up on some scaffolding when he fell off and landed twenty feet below on some concrete. He was hurt pretty bad. Medical attention is out of the question especially when he is a pastor. Just taking it easy at home and prayer was the only remedy allowed him. After a while he started feeling better, enough to take two trips. One trip was to encourage the congregation in Mexico, and the other trip, to encourage the outreach in the Philippines.

Upon coming back home he decided that he felt good enough to go back to work. Doing that however became a horror story. He acquired a hernia the size of a volley ball! Imagine holding nearly your entire intestines in your hands in front of your stomach! He lived like that waiting for God to heal him. All his relatives were called to pay their last regards to him in case God chose to take him to Heaven.

Two Church "Brothers" decided to help God out. Remember that this group does not believe in medicine or doctors, but now they will attempt a doctor thing. They will try to gently push this hernia and all his guts back inside! Common sense could have said that there could be major complications. There was. A blood vessel ruptured and he bled to death right before their eyes, leaving behind his wife and six children. His youngest child was eight days old who will never know her (I think daughter) Daddy because of their doctrine.

This cult encourages joy at funerals since the deceased has gone to heaven. It would be unnatural for a spouse to sing at her husband's funeral, but Gerry's wife did. I wonder how much the cult has to pump somebody up to do something like that. Whatever the situation the cult will completely surround or totally engulf one of their members when trouble hits. The person will have 24/7 attention as long as needed to get over it. I asked an "insider" one time if they think that my wife will ever come back to me. Their response was that there is a constant supply of "Saints" around her to never allow her to think for herself. They protect their members to the extreme.

Sunflower Seeds

Traveling across the Country at great distances I acquired the desire for sunflower seeds. Driving for hours can fatigue the mind and decrease alertness. I enjoy crunching on ice and also seeds. Miles fly by as you concentrate with a mouthful of seeds at positioning a single seed, cracking it, chewing the inside, and spitting out the shell in an empty cup. Because of that pastime I usually had a bag of seeds in my vehicle.

When Stevie was about two or maybe three I had an incident with him. At the time I was already involved with the cult. Our little chapel building was out in the country on a dirt road. Our vehicles were parked just outside the door. Steve fell asleep in my arms during the sermon. My arms were getting sore so I thought that I would lay Steve down inside my van just a few yards away which I did.

I went back inside to listen to the rest of the service keeping close watch on my van also. The service ended and the entire congregation stepped outside to enjoy this beautiful early summer day. I think it was about June. We all enjoyed this new established congregation, and we were part of it! All the rules were not really mentioned yet, although I knew they practiced and preached

Divine Healing. Not going to doctors was not forced upon us yet. Life was great!

Soon my family approached our vehicle to drive home. That is when we noticed that Stevie had awakened and was eating my sunflower seeds, shells and all. Mommy took the bag away from my little rascal not realizing that he had another handful of them. We left the chapel and did not even get a mile down the road when Stevie started choking. Once again, mommy to the rescue! She grabbed him and pounded his back.

All the seeds appeared to be out but he instantly had a wheezing in his throat that he did not have before. We drove home and I called the hospital with some questions. Could there possibly be some seeds still in his windpipe which causes the wheezing? They assured me that it is absolutely not possible because even if it was the tiniest speck he would be in convulsions with the task of breathing. He probably had a shell cut his throat which causes the wheezing.

That Sunday before the evening church service, Stevie still was not better, and complained of pain incapable of signifying where, how, or why. So I complied with the teachings of the church in the area of Divine Healing. I let him get anointed and prayed for, and then waited for his healing. Days turned into weeks, and weeks turned into months. There was some kind of meeting in Ohio about two months after it happened. Concerned, I asked for several ministers to anoint and pray for him there. Also from my viewpoint I now believed that there would be a healing because there were several pastors.

Not seeing any change for the months that followed, I started to wonder if what I was being told was actually what the Bible was saying. The wheezing continued and at least five months had gone by. Every time I brought up his condition, people responded that Stevie had asthma. I refused to believe that because the wheezing started instantly when he was choking on the seeds. They disagreed with my evaluation.

The Oklahoma meeting arrived each year during the Thanksgiving week and once again we were "forcefully encouraged" to attend that meeting. At that meeting I remember holding my baby and letting some people listen to his breathing. They commented that his breathing sounded like the snoring of an old man. One of the people that said that was Paulette whom I mentioned earlier in this book who was excommunicated sometime after that. Why all these months and no change?

Once again I brought him to the altar and had several ministers pray for him. Later I was reproved that I brought the same case to the Lord twice. That is inappropriate according to them. For myself it seemed more like the parable of the woman that persistently begged the wicked Judge for a favor. The woman received because she would not quit asking. Luke 18:2-5.

Emotionally bothered, I brought my family back from Oklahoma. I mentioned my predicament to my sister. She told me that one of her daughters fell on her back from off something and had a wheezing also. My sister took her daughter to a chiropractor who straightened out her spine, which cured the wheezing.

Tired of waiting six months for a healing, I took Stevie to the chiropractor. Before the practitioner even touched him, he showed us a drawing of the human body. Each vertebrae affected a different part of the body and certain organs. If this specific vertebrae is out of line, (he named it with a number) then that vertebrae can prevent healing in the throat area. He told us that he suspected when mommy pounded the back, she removed the shells, but then also beat the vertebrae out of alignment. The body then is prevented from repairing itself. He told us what he suspected, which vertebrae, and also what would happen after he corrected it, before he even took my child. He told us that because it had been six months since the incident. He could pop the bones back into place, however, because of the lengthy time of wrong alignment, things might reverse again to wrong alignment and he would need a second follow up to make sure it stays where it is supposed to. Also, he told me not to worry about the child running a slight fever and sleeping much more for the next day or two. That is normal for the body will start healing.

He took my baby from me. Sure enough, the exact vertebrae

*

that he mentioned was out. There was another one out too. Bouncing my child carefully between his hands in a upright position we heard two separate and distinct pops. He reassured us that he had the back bone aligned, and said he'd see us next week. Amazing! My son ran a fever and slept a lot. Within two weeks the wheezing was gone forever. My Stevie breathed like a normal child and also the way I remembered him before the incident with the seeds. My thoughts logged something into my mind that confirmed a belief. There was a time and place for doctors and chiropractors instead of this church's practice of Divine Healing. I started concentrating on several cases that I saw presented before that church and their ministers. I analyzed the results of the ones that I could. I never saw them heal anybody the way that Jesus and his disciples did. Every "healing" that they gloated about was a natural healing that required time.

I presented a question to Pat one time. I started by saying; suppose a Saint, a Sinner, and a stray dog got sick all with the same sickness. The Saint gets anointed and prayed for by this group and in three days he feels healed. The Sinner is sick also and goes to the doctor and in three days he feels better. The stray dog just lies around, doesn't eat, but in three days gets up and starts running around again because the sickness has taken its course. I asked him which of the three got a Divine Healing like the one the Bible talks about. Are all of them or none of them divine healed because they all ended up with the same three day outcome? He did not answer my question but said that I had deep spiritual problems because I was questioning the Church's doctrine.

Patrick and the Lima bean

Being in the tree cutting business definitely has disadvantages when you live in town. City ordinances would not allow stockpiling the entire backyard full of firewood. I had no lot in the country where I could take the wood to either. Putting an ad in the local newspaper for free firewood solved the problem temporarily. Some people would just grab the pieces that only weigh about fifty pounds or less and leave the rest. Often people would reject certain species of trees or certain locations and distances from their place. The wood on the other side of town became my problem again.

Mentioning my problem to Pat, my pastor, started him thinking of how he could benefit from my dilemma. He offered to take every piece off of my hands. Placing an ad in the paper for cut, split, and delivered firewood for sale quickly started the operation going.

Pat was very familiar with shop tools and safety since he taught shop class in an Illinois public school. In order to be the teacher he had to know and teach the safety involving tools. Plenty of cut up firewood was already on the ground for his taking when he rolled up with his pickup and a trailer. Helping him was his young teenage son. Pat placed a large chunk of wood on the splitter while Johnny pulled the lever back and forth as required. That is a safety rule violation for two people operating the splitter like this because one person does not know what the other person is planning on doing. The person that handles the wood may want to rotate the wood slightly just as Johnny thinks it is time to pull the lever. Pull the lever at the wrong time and the knife splits the wood and anything else in the way as the hydraulic cylinder pushes the knife through. Accidents are prone to happen.

It was in the winter months and snow was on the ground. Their system seemed to be working smoothly and the pickup and trailer was filling up with their first load. I kept working at taking the tree down for the firewood removal was no longer my responsibility.

This might just work, or did I think that too soon?

Suddenly Pat pulled back fast and yelled out "Johnny!" real loud. Instantly I saw blood dripping on the snow. Red snow was increasing rapidly. The operation shut down immediately to see what had happened. Pat had decided to move the piece of wood a little different on an afterthought just as Johnny thought he was ready. He pulled the wood splitter lever just as his Dad stuck his hand back in to rotate the wood just slightly more. The knife caught him right behind his fingernail of his longest finger and sheared it off. The tip of his bone was sticking out a little bit.

Things were not very funny at that moment anymore. Pat was taking advantage of the snowbank by sticking his finger into it. It was time to unhook and take him home. I thought back about the other pastor whom I called "Sam" with the nail in his hand. This time however, Pat had no intention of going to the hospital. We piled into my van and headed for his house. The entire trip he was praying furiously out loud, and mentioned that it was beginning to hurt worse.

Imagine getting your finger tip squeezed off and absolutely no pain killer, medication, or doctor! The only thing is prayer which appeared by his volume that it was not helping much. All he could do was verbalize his prayer of desire without ever acquiring any miraculous result. A week later Pat confronted me in trying to find out what I thought. I told him that I did not agree in calling his endurance of this accident as Divine Healing. After all, his bone was sticking out a little bit which could cause problems.

After about a month he came to me entirely confident that he received divine healing. He made a big deal about showing me that the flesh has started to grow over his bone. Wow! I saw a dog one time lose his leg in a large trap. It too healed over and the dog got used to running on three legs. Did it receive divine healing also?

After taking Pat home I had to return to the job site to at least retrieve my equipment. Back at the wood splitter we noticed the torn up glove. Inside I saw the white and frozen fingertip. It looked like a Lima bean.

You would like to know, how could anyone want to join

anything like this? Anybody stupid enough to join themselves to rules like that deserve to get what the cult hands out to them, right? Is that what you are thinking? If I would have known everything that I have mentioned so far in this book, I never would have attended even the first gathering with any cult members in it either. So how then did I get trapped into it? I will answer that in the next chapter.

Thank God for White Blood Cells!

My skepticism to the cult's version of divine healing got me in a lot of trouble. As I mentioned earlier, I started taking each miracle of healing of Jesus and also of his disciples afterward, and placed each one separately on a colored recipe card. I confronted Pat O'Shea on it, but who then passed it onto the master mind, Danny Layne, in California? I was at the California camp meeting, I believe it was in March, when I was confronted by Danny, and was ordered to his private minister's building. Once in a room he criticized me of my resistance to truth. I didn't think I was resisting truth. He clarified then what he was referring to. "Just because you don't see or understand divine healing does NOT mean it isn't happening" he said. To that I agreed.

"Then what seems to be the problem for my resistance?", he questioned me.

I start to expound on what I felt the Bible taught on healing. Every healing that Jesus did, I believe was instantaneous, while everything I witnessed in this church was a natural healing. I hate it when it is called a divine healing. The cult was insulting my God when they give him several days or weeks to heal, and when the slow change of improvement finally happens, they say it was divine healing. God is not that weak! He could do it in the blink of an eye. Call it a natural healing from God and I can accept that easily, but don't insult God by saying he needs time to slowly make a change.

"You are not reading your Bible" he challenged me. "The ten leapers were healed as they went!"

My response to that was that Jesus was in the same city where the church (temple) was and that is where the lepers were ordered to go. How long does it take to walk maybe a mile? One leper came back to thank Jesus for healing him. How many days, weeks, or months did Jesus have to stand there for his return? The only way that verse makes any sense is if the lepers left a few hundred yards away and suddenly they noticed that they had been healed instantaneously. In frustration Danny finished by challenging me, if I thank God for white blood cells?

Divine Healing and white blood cells, are not the same thing and I believe he didn't appreciate the challenge I gave him. I was a "Free Thinker" and needed to be gotten rid of.

One time Pat and I were arguing about divine healing. I do not have a doubt that it happens, but I doubt that he has been around it to give me an example where he has witnessed it. "Since you believe that you have been among divine healing of what I am describing the bible times had, give me an example", I asked him. He then gave me two examples that sounded to me like the actual experience that I was talking about. The one example was when he witnessed it in a former church that he attended in Chicago. The second example is also of another church that he attended in Guthrie, Oklahoma. That seemed ironic to me!

I then asked him, "Why did you choose two examples that seemed genuine, but both cases are from two different churches that you call Babylon? Why did you not give me an example within this One and Only True Church? Does not this church have examples of divine healing, and only the ones whom you call Babylon have that gift?" I left him speechless and angry with me.

Safety and Health Threat Issue

Wisconsin Dells has a lot of attractions to draw people to this area. Unable to participate with most of the activities due to this cult's condemnation on almost everything, I took my children one time viewing of these forbidden things. We had gone on a boat ride earlier and were now just trying to find something else to use up our time that I had with them. It was a very hot day with a temperature right around ninety degrees.

Dress code is standard regardless what the temperature is. All my children seemed to be miserably hot with those long clothes of several layers and dark colored fabric. Suddenly my youngest, Bethany, arched her back as if she was going into a convulsion. Her face was clammy but slightly sweaty. She was somewhat crying but mostly displaying hysterical emotions. Is she having a heat stroke? I was trying to decide what to do as we rushed back to our vehicle.

Once at the van I knew I had to try cooling Bethany down first. I gave her some water even though she did not want to drink much. To me she seemed hot and I suspected that she was on the edge of a heat stroke or heat exhaustion. I started pouring the water on top of her despite her resistance to it. The cult has influenced them to believe that they can't get wet like that, for the wet clothing will reveal immodesty.

Then I started opening up her vest and outside layers just to see that there were more layers beneath. She must have had on at least four layers of clothing in this incredible heat. Even the military understands the dangers of heat and allows their people to loosen up the uniforms to ensure ventilation. However, this cult does not have that allowance ever.

When I tried making an issue out of what happened in this story, the cult turned the blame on me for not providing plenty of liquids to Bethany.

They accused me that her convulsions had nothing to do with her overly multi-layered dress code, but was entirely written off as my negligence of not supplying enough water.

Vaccination

Because the cult refuses to use medicine, it is obvious of how they will stand on immunization. I believe every child in the cult is not immunized whose parents have been with that group before the birth of that child. I find it ironic that by law the common person must have his child immunized, but then the entire system of the Kenosha Court will favor the parent who has refused to concede to the law. For over six years now, the judges, attorneys, and the Guardian Ad-Litium, (GAL- children's court appointed attorney), has declared that my children are best off in the cares of the mother that is involved in this cult.

There was a measles outbreak the Spring of 2008, in this country. At the time I was thinking of what would happen if an outbreak would attack this cult. In one day it could spread throughout the entire congregation. If there was a disease, the mouth-to-mouth kissing alone, would pass it to every member on just one Sunday.

If one of their members steps on a rusty nail, they would not get a Tetanus shot. They would just get prayed for by a group of ministers that I have never witnessed a divine healing from. If the injured could be naturally healed, they will be all right. However, if it becomes an infection that would lead to death, they probably will die.

I knew Agatha as a young teenager. She had stayed at our house a few days to help Shereen with her daily duties. Everything is a secret of what happened to the outsiders like me. However, placing bits and pieces together I embrace the idea that something must have happened in Mexico. The cult does a lot of traveling to countries that have certain diseases like malaria. The members do not get immunized for any of that. I heard Agatha went to Mexico and acquired some disease. By being in this cult, I am sure she didn't seek any medical attention. The outcome is that she died young while still in her twenties, adding to the skeletons in the "closet" of this cult.

CHAPTER 6
MY STORY OF ENTRAPMENT

I was raised on a farm in Hinckley, Minnesota, one of seven children born to Edmund and Ruth Tocholke. Both were German immigrants who brought with them to this country little more than the lives that were spared during WWII. I recall hearing stories from Oma, my grandmother, of the bombs and shrapnel, the burial afterwards of military men, and the butchering of the military horses that were killed in battle. Often times that was the only food supply they had.

As a married man I brought Oma to be part of my family for up to a week per month at times. She accompanied us on many family outings. During one particular excursion, I stopped to show my children an old army tank that was on display. To us it was a real thrill to crawl underneath and then into the belly trap door. Oma, however, was disturbed. She had seen enough tanks in her lifetime, recalling seeing them run over people in the streets of Germany, turning them into mush.

That night I was awakened by the sound of my eighty year old Oma screaming, followed by a thud. I found her on the floor, bewildered and unsure of how to get back into the bed from which she had fallen. I scooped her up like a small child and laid her back in the bed. I spent a few moments calming her and she recalled that the dream had been of Russian soldiers, with rape and murder on their minds. She had barely escaped their pursuit when she fell out of the bed.

Oma's stories had a great impact on my life, especially in matters concerning the waste of food. I was raised to at least try a little bit of whatever was being offered, but if I filled up my plate I was required to eat it. To this day even if the food isn't my favorite, I will still manage to choke it down. When I see people piling food onto their plates at buffets, only to leave half of it to be thrown out,

I am reminded of the hardships that my grandparents faced living in a war torn country.

Oma's stories also affected my perception of life and mortality. War does not increase the mortality rate, nor does disease or terrorism; death is one hundred percent inevitable. Coming to this realization at a young age led me to search for a solution to this problem; I became sensitive to the idea of life after death.

Although there are many unpleasant events that make up my childhood, I have fond memories of farm life and I wouldn't trade it for anything. As a positive minded child I tended to focus on the fun I had. The combination of fun, adventure, and creative expression with work, pain and hardship makes for a character that is not easily broken. At a young age I had convinced my parents that I didn't know how to work the milking machines, and that important job was delegated to my older sister. I started driving a tractor at about the age of eight, preferring that job to the cows and their strict milking schedule. I was also assigned to the less stringent task of feeding and watering the animals,- the cattle, pigs and poultry. We often had a couple horses on the farm as well.

With six more siblings there was never a shortage of things to do. We built forts out in the hay, rolled down a hill in a tractor tire (but only once!) and even used cow pies to decorate rocks in the fields. We destroyed cornfields building forts within it, flattening everything in sight. During the spring thaw and flooding, we jumped into the river that ran through Dad's land, surprisingly none of us suffered hypothermia. Once, as Dad was taking a nap on the sofa, I brought our Shetland pony into the house. The surprised look on Dad's face when the pony's muzzle woke him up was worth it.

Having no television in the house, we would invent games to play on the farm. One of those games was called Fire Drill. We would empty the contents of the house out onto the lawn. How quickly we were able to reload the furnishings into the house when we saw our parents coming home, less than a mile down the road.

On Sundays, we gathered in the basement of my grandpa's house. Sitting there with my aunts, uncles and cousins, we listened to sermons recorded on reel to reel tapes. The tapes were shipped from the German Church of God (Gemeinde Gottes) in Edmonton Alberta Canada. As a child I found these basement church services to be boring. The voices on the tape belonged to people far away. I couldn't relate to the singing or preaching at all. It wasn't until my aunt Johanna and my cousins took me to the German church in Winnipeg, when I was thirteen or fourteen, that I was able to connect with the sermons on tape. I saw people standing in front of the congregation to sing songs. The preaching was done in the German style, which lacked the emotion and fervor that I would experience in later years, but I was finally able to interact with other worshipers.

I didn't attend kindergarten but went straight to first grade. I remember sitting in class, unable to understand what anyone was saying, and no one being able to understand me either. I didn't have a German translator. The communication barrier enabled for future withdrawal into myself, to the point that I was ignoring my own emotional needs. This was a setback which shaped my thinking for many years.

In more than one instance the language barrier caused me embarrassment. In my first few months of public schooling, unable to voice my needs to the teacher, and in need of the restroom, I wet my pants while seated at my desk. The only English word for liquid that I could think of was water. I used the word when the teacher indicated the puddle under my chair with dismay. I was quickly labeled by my classmates as the stupid kid.

Later during that first year I was confronted by two second grade bullies. They were just two little boys, but to my first grade eyes they were giants. With the few English words that I had acquired, I deciphered what it was they wanted in exchange for not beating me up,- toys. The deal was that if I brought them my toys they would be my friends; however, if I failed to relinquish my possessions, they would beat me up every day until I brought what they wanted.

I was faced with two problems. One, I didn't want to be beaten up by the two second graders. The second problem was, coming from a poor family. I didn't have many personal toys. How would I sneak my few possessions out of the house without my parents noticing?

Instead of taking the risk of being caught by my parents, I spent the next few days hanging around the playground supervisor. She urged me to go play, but I had no desire to use the monkey bars or swings. I knew that the older boys would want to play "Punch the stupid kid." I didn't find the game to be any fun. For the next twelve years I spent the majority of my time running whenever faced with conflict.

I made it through to high school unscathed. I did have one run-in in my junior year. I was in need of the bathroom and just as I was finishing up the same two boys walked in. They were seniors then and able to instill the same old fear in me as when I was a first grader. They blocked the door standing shoulder to shoulder and one of them said, "Now look at what we have here. Where are the toys?"

The next ten seconds took hours to go by. I thought I was mincemeat. They canceled their bluff by elbowing each other and proceeded into the bathroom. On this one occasion I did not obey my mom's rule of washing my hands, but immediately fled, completely shaken.

I was a late bloomer, barely over five feet tall when I graduated, and gaining another six inches when I was nineteen or twenty. Being the runt hardly gave me opportunity to try bullying for myself; even most of the girls were taller than I was back then.

Though my parents worked hard to provide for our basic needs, we grew up in a cold house with no insulation in the walls. The pipes often froze, nearly every night, during the harsh Minnesota winters. Though we had an indoor toilet, the septic system usually froze up by mid-winter, forcing us to use the outhouse for the remaining long months.

Another character forming experience from my childhood was the clothes I had to wear. Mom did a lot of the shopping for us kids at yard sales and thrift stores. We wore the clothing that the previous owner had deemed unacceptable for themselves.

I was ashamed of the patterns Mom chose from the limited selection she had. I hated wearing striped pants and plaid shirts. One day Mom came home with a real find. It was a shirt with a horse pattern on it. I loved horses and was excited about this particular shirt.

The very next day I proudly wore the shirt with one of the two pair of solid colored pants I owned. Once I was on the school bus, my cousin Ron pointed out how baggy the sleeves were. It was true I could fit both arms into one of the sleeves. I became self-conscious. During the school day I kept trying to roll the extra fabric and hold it under my arm, close to my side. Why did they sew so much fabric in the sleeves? I wasn't Popeye!

When I got home I approached Mom and asked about the sleeves. She studied the shirt and pointed out that the buttons were on the wrong side too. It was then that we realized that I had been wearing a woman's blouse all day, and not a shirt!

The animals on the farm never noticed my second-hand clothes, or that I was smaller than most other boys my age. They never ridiculed me for the way I spoke. I found peace in the solitude of crawling into the dog's house or falling asleep with the calves.

When I was fifteen I made a decision that would impact the rest of my life. I found someone, besides the animals, who would never ridicule or put me down. That person was Jesus Christ. My Aunt Johanna invited an English speaking Church of God preacher to hold a week-long revival meeting in Hinckley. A bus load of people arrived, representing several southern states. They rented the VFW hall and held meetings every night in my home town. I remember listening to everything they sang, all of the words preached, and feeling emotions that I had never encountered before. I was experiencing what I heard referred to as the old time conviction. Each night after the sermon was done, the altar-calling songs were being sung and I couldn't sing. If I had opened my mouth I would have broken into tears.

For all of the emotions that I was feeling I was still too scared to go up to the altar with everyone watching me. All of my encounters with ridicule at the hands of others taught me to shy away from the attention of others. By the end of the week I had formulated a plan to speak with the missionary about praying together privately. I approached the man after the service outside with questions about my salvation. He immediately sensed my shyness, put his arm around my shoulder and led me to the front of the church exactly where I didn't want to go, but now it didn't matter, because I received a peace at the altar that I will always remember.

After my decision to turn my life over to God and Christ I started reading the Bible. Some might have thought me a religious fanatic. Kids at school tried to make a spectacle of me praying before lunch at school. I was mocked for my faith, sometimes with words and sometimes with physical assault.

I continued studying what God calls our "Duty of Conduct," and strove to adhere to His word. I wanted to live each day the way I felt He wanted me to, not just on Sundays. As an example, the absolute of not stealing was one that I strove to abide even in situations that other so-called Christians may have looked the other way. For instance one time, I had just finished fueling up my car, when gas prices were still about a dollar a gallon. I ran inside to pay the cashier. I handed her a ten dollar bill. I grabbed my change without looking and headed back out. When I checked the change I had been handed, I saw that it was eleven dollars, change for a twenty. I turned back and placed the money back on the counter. There are many people who would have seen this human mistake as a sign of good fortune and placed the money into their wallet. For myself, I can't let a dishonest penny keep me out of heaven.

It seemed to my young mind that many people were living the lives they wanted during the week and showed up at church on Sundays telling, everyone what a good Christian they were. I refused to live that double life, making my belief a constant and obvious feature in my daily living.

I learned about marriage and love from my parents. I don't remember them ever calling each other by their names or anything other than "Schatze," which is a German word meaning "sweetheart, or precisely, "treasure." It was normal for us to see

Mom and dad kissing and hugging, or Mom sitting on Dad's lap. The children came second to one another. For the twenty-four unmarried years of my life, I assumed that the definition of marriage was the picture they presented, with little to be improved upon.

I met Shereen in 1984. She was working as a teacher in a Catholic grade school. I was doing custodial work for the church and school. We didn't begin dating right way. When I inquired into her status she responded that she was in a relationship. It wasn't until many months later that I learned she was available and I was able to ask her for a date on Valentine's Day 1985. We went to a restaurant and spent an hour talking. With the exception of just a few days, I saw her every day after that until we were married six months later.

Using the model set before me by my parents, I started married life with Shereen in August of 1985. Shereen and I had gathered together our childhood pictures to put together as a slide show, to be presented to the guests at our wedding. The divergence in lifestyles was apparent in the photos. One slide of Shereen, all clean and prissy, and then one of me riding a horse, dressed in rags. Another photo, this one a professional shot of her and my new in-laws, followed by the informal snapshot of me standing with my family, dirty from a hard day's work, standing next to a broken down pick up.

Compared to my impoverished childhood, Shereen had grown up in the lap of luxury. I was unaccustomed to the needs of a woman raised as one of four children, in a family in which much importance is placed upon material things. My mom was content living in an old house and later a run-down used trailer home. I built a brand new home for Shereen to live in, wanting to fulfill her every want. Growing up I was a loner, not in need of company of others to stay content. Shereen on the other hand was more outgoing and did not enjoy being alone. This need for constant attention made life with the cult even more appealing for her.

A few years later while I was in jail I studied the difference in people. Man has created jails to be uncomfortable to most people.

Most people fall into despair when isolated. Because of this mental state, jails contain 6x8 rooms for isolating the bad people. I saw a man who was taken to the "hole" for a petty violation. He snapped within a couple of hours and tried committing suicide. The guards found him hanging from a bed sheet, unconscious.

After being shut out of the cult that had become my life, I'm sure they thought that the loneliness would overcome me and I would beg them to take me back. But I had learned as a child to adapt to being the outsider and spent enough time alone to learn to be comfortable with myself.

My Mom never worked outside of the home while my siblings and I were growing up. I wanted the same for my wife. Shereen stayed home raising and schooling our children.

Right after we were married we began "church shopping." We lived in Brooklyn Park, MN at the time, which is near Minneapolis. We eventually moved to Spooner, Wisconsin, where we settled on a small, conservative, non-denominational church. The congregation was made up of very helpful and neighborly people. The pastor and his family were sincere.

There were a few minor things about doctrine at that church that I didn't agree with, but then, there isn't any such thing as a perfect church. However, we soon met a group that claimed they were.

It was my cousin that told me of a man that lived near Chicago. He had been up a few times to preach in my cousin's church. The man's name was Patrick O'Shea. He was described to me as an aggressive warrior when it came to passing out religious tracts or preaching on street corners. I was impressed with the courage of this man, and accepted the invitation to hear him preach at my cousin's church.

I didn't agree with all of the radical methods Patrick O'Shea used, but nonetheless felt a challenge to be more assertive with the gospel. When I finally met him, he was kind and courteous, if a little froward and pushy.

He was not unreserved in the asking questions that I at times felt were too invasive. He seemed to probe for how I lived, my prayer life, my bible readings and what God was showing me. If he needed to know something for his mission, he just asked. I didn't have any secrets and so was not offended by his questioning.

Upon first meeting Patrick O'Shea, he right away invited us to visit him near Chicago, Illinois. The following spring, my family took up his offer and went to Chicago. We visited the zoos and museums during the day, and in the evenings we spent our time with the O'Sheas until morning. One thing the reader needs to understand is that what I already mentioned in this book developed over several years. The issues that I mentioned were not there at this point, and the rules were either secret, or kept from us, or had not been developed yet. Most of the rules developed from year to year. The O'Shea family had just gotten involved with the COGR. They had not yet fully conformed to all the strange beliefs and attitudes either. Shortly thereafter though, I received some shirts of Pat O'Shea, which were not appropriate to the CoGR. They were mildly striped, like a white shirt with faintly light blue stripes which were not permissible. I questioned that, but it was shrugged away as just personal preference. Months later this so called "personal preference," confronted me on my turf.

The only way that someone can comprehend exactly what the sub-surface spirit of this group is, is to be part of it for a while. Until that happens a full understanding of how a group can all silently agree or disagree is a mystery. The subtle attitudes and actions only show up after you have officially testified that you have taken a stand with them. The disgusting thing about it is that they will say that it is the Holy Spirit that conforms their members to all the same dress, similar to the 1800's type of apparel. Reality though is the sermons, Bible studies, and subtle hints or comments are that people are flirting with the world and the enemy. That knowledge then changes and conforms the members to one code. The mild rejection from the cult, concerning with non-conformity to the issues, does not get presented to visitors or new members. However, as the months go by the new member must conform or they will sense the rejection in very subtle ways.

Years earlier, before all the extreme issues began, the O'Shea family was nothing more than just a conservative family. He was very outgoing when it came to handing out tracts. It seemed to me that every person in sight must take a tract from him. I was embarrassed about the pushy way he thrust the pamphlets at every passerby. This behavior did not mesh with my country upbringing. I thought that due to the people of Chicago which seemed so calloused to religion, that this was what must be needed there.

Near the end of this visit, another invitation was extended. This time we were asked to attend at the camp meeting in Ohio that summer. I expressed that we would not be able to join them because money was an issue. Immediately, money was offered in order for my family to be able to join the congregation at the camp meeting that summer. Food and accommodations were also included. I wish I would have understood then what all would transpire after that and how new rules would be added from year to year.

When we arrived that summer in Ohio, we were treated like celebrities. Everyone went out of their way to greet us and make sure we were comfortable. This was certainly a change from growing up avoiding people, quite opposite of the experiences of my school days. I did not realize at the time that this was a ploy used by this cult to keep prospective members coming back.

The style of dress worn by the men in the congregation was strange to me; a long sleeved white shirt, with dark suit. But to the former boy who had worn a woman's blouse to school, the clothing was hardly a deterrent.

Within a few months one of their pastors moved up by us near Spooner, Wisconsin. For about two years we had a small fellowship with a few other people joining us. Each year Danny Layne was adding more rules for us to follow. I will elaborate more on him now and will continue my entrapment story in chapter eight. The next chapter happened over several years, and some of the stories occurred after I was already in their "frying pan".

CHAPTER 7

<u>DANNY LAYNE- THE MASTER MIND</u>

Daniel Layne spent 19 years, according to his self-published pamphlet "He Lifted Me Out," shooting drugs until he had "used up every vein" in his body. At the age of 36, after attempting to chop off his arms with a meat cleaver, God spoke to him saying, "If you will give me your life, I will save you."

Danny became part of the Church of God in California, with the Headquarters in Oklahoma. But left in 1989 after concluding that the teachings of the church were "too liberal." He started his own church in Aylmer, Ontario, Canada. There he met the Hildebrandt brothers; Peter, Henry, and David. They were Mexican Mennonites, once associated with the Church of God, who also believed that the teachings were too lenient. The Church of God Restoration grew and according to their website has congregations in the US, Canada, Mexico, Europe, Africa and Philippines.

What new members don't realize is that Danny is the "invisible" master mind and controller behind most of the decisions. The member might not like the way their pastor is trying to control them, but he is only the puppet doing what Danny told him to do.

One thing that amazed or shocked me is that Danny has NO "Equal". The common member of this cult was expected to seek the altar often. The members which where looked up to the most by the ministers were the ones that did exactly that. However, the ministers were seldom seen there. And yet during all the years I witnessed the procedure, every time someone went to the altar a minister or altar worker of equal or greater spirituality would join them there to pray with them and give them spiritual advice.

One time Danny preached an emotionally strong message. Upon finishing it, he walked from behind the pulpit and knelt at the altar. The entire place was solemn and people filled the altar. Every seeker received an altar worker. Throughout the years, this is the only time I ever saw Danny Layne at the altar. The amazing thing, he was the only person that didn't have an altar worker. There was no one equal or superior to him. It seemed strange to me to see someone at the altar with everyone else but no one was beside him.

The cult will argue that Danny is not the "Top Dog", but might point out another minister. After being part of the cult for several years, I know that to be just an evasive tactic or ploy. Every year at the Ohio camp meeting, the large group had to assemble for a professional photographer. I usually special ordered a 10x13 photo of the group, since the crowd was so large and actually seeing faces clearly on a smaller photo was difficult.

One thing that seemed very odd to me though is what took place during that day. A very tall step ladder was used by the photographer so he could capture everyone for the group photo. He took another picture of just the small children, another one of the young people maybe up to twenty-five years of age, and then young married couples also were a special bracket. A picture of the ministers and their spouses was I think the last bracket. After all the various poses and multiple pictures were taken, the photographer left to develop the proofs.

What seemed odd to me is that in a few hours when the photographer came back with the proofs, he was ordered to go straight to Danny Layne for evaluation. He was THE top dog then to accept and reject which proofs would be available to the congregation and which would not be. The excuse was that Danny had a rough past and his heroin abuse ruined his body especially his eyes. The first few pictures with a flash camera will irritate his eyes and they will start squinting and watering profusely. Therefore, Danny has superior right to reject any pictures where he is facially distorted. It does not matter if any of the rest of the congregation or group has their eyes shut or whatever, as long as he is presentable. He had control even on the pictures he was not in. Why should that be?

I was also amused at the acting performance that he can do. He would be preaching on something, and suddenly he would turn emotional. "I was lost in sin: After nineteen years of drugs, I had used up nearly every vein in my body," he cried. "But then Jesus came to me and told me, that if I give myself to him, that he will clean up my life!" He gets emotional and tears stream down his face. As if on cue, others in the congregation pull out their handkerchiefs and start wiping their eyes. I believe it was in the early 80's when this "conversion" happened, but he could still bring the congregation to tears with that same speech of his. He developed that act of emotions to perfection.

Another thing that I found peculiar was how he operated under church money. After his recovery from drug addiction, I heard the government gave him a monthly check if he stayed off of drugs. For many years he would cash that free money, even though he was getting some church money on the side. I witnessed that in Spooner, Wisconsin, our beginning congregation provided Danny's airfare from California and five hundred dollars to hold daily services for us for a full week. Within the last few years however, when the government wanted to investigate his financial activities, he declined accepting their money anymore.

I heard from a reliable source that they witnessed Danny taking money right out of the church's offering box to get himself a seventy dollar sweater. His assumption I suppose is that it is being used for church purposes since he will wear it to church services, even though the IRS would see it as personal use. Throughout the eight years that I was with them, I don't ever remember getting a receipt for all the offering money that I gave.

The camp meetings are a big expense. I have a suspicion that Danny gets his room for free while the other members pay the percentage or divided amount that would pay for the rental of the grounds. I sure wish the IRS could investigate into the legality of their operation. Unfortunately, the IRS can't have a lot of flexibility since the cult uses and abuses the system when it deals with freedom of religion. That right protects the cult even though they are involved in child abuse, medical neglect, or tax fraud.

Danny is open or reveals his attitude toward certain people if he believes he can trust you. James was a pastor whom I liked but was inexperienced as a leader or speaker. One time he elaborated on a personal story that he had experienced for almost an hour. I had heard his story several times by now and felt that he had wasted an hour of my life while he presented it as a Sunday morning church sermon.

When I approached Danny with my opinion of it, he mocked it and James in a certain fashion. With his chuckle and short comments, I knew what his attitude was toward James himself. After I was abandoned by my wife, condemned and shunned by the cult members, I related what Danny said and did, to James who was still in the cult. He approached Danny on it and I believe there was some denial of the truth, but it allowed James to see the real Danny and his cult. He is no longer a member of that group.

I vividly recall one message that Danny was preaching about avoiding the presence of evil by deftly evading time with your relatives that are not in this cult. He bragged how he has taken all the small children of his California congregation, loaded them into the large church van, and took them all to Dairy Queen. His point of bragging spiked when he mentioned that those children's own grandparents would never be allowed to even do that to their grandchildren. We need to guard our children from anyone outside of this One, True Church, especially from the relatives.

This story comes from a couple whom I believe to be a very reliable source. They were at a camp meeting a few years before I knew anything of Danny Layne and his group. It was in the afternoon during the children's Bible school classes, when my friend whom I will call "Jack" and his wife were in their cabin resting for evening service. They woke up when they heard a tussle or skirmish outside their door. Curious they tiptoed to the door to see what is going on. Very quietly they cracked the door open just enough to see.

Danny was furious with a small child. He was hitting the small boy and then threw him on the ground. Once the boy was on the ground the witnesses couldn't believe their eyes, Danny started kicking him. He picked the boy back off the ground and hit him several times again before throwing him back on the ground for more kicking. This was repeated several times. Later Jack found out why the "discipline" had taken place. The little boy had refused to participate with the other children when they needed to sing, "Jesus loves me this I know"!

Danny is still the "Top Dog" in that cult. The witnessing couple is no longer part of that cult. And the boy, well, I don't know who he was but, he had the love of Jesus beat into him.

Jason and Crystal were a couple that had attended our Kenosha congregation for a while but never seemed to agree to be consistent members at the same time. If Crystal was actively coming to service, Jason couldn't find the need to attend this church. Then it would flop the other way and Jason would come testifying that he is happy to be amongst God's chosen people, and Crystal would stay at home believing this way to be in error.

It was during the time that Jason was following what the cult was teaching when I witnessed this. Camp meeting in Ohio had arrived and we as the congregation were all ordered to attend this meeting for the sake of our soul. Jason also made the plans and caught a ride with the O'Shea's. There was a cruel order that came down from the ministry that Jason had to do. He followed through with the orders. Before he left that night with the van, he took the car keys and all of the money. Without money or a way to get anywhere, Crystal was left helplessly at home.

Once we arrived in Ohio Jason came to me and told me what happened. He told me that Crystal called the campground and got a hold of him. She cried on the phone and told him that she made a mistake and that she wishes she was down here too. Jason asked me if I would even consider taking him up there to bring her back down. I said I would do that if he wanted to.

Word of our intentions got slipped to Danny Layne and he called both of us immediately. He said, "If she insisted on losing or rejecting her ride when the Saints left Kenosha, let her figure out herself now how she is going to get down here." He then demanded that we were not allowed to leave the camp meeting to go back to Kenosha. That was a forceful order. In my mind I wondered why all the dirty play of taking all the money? That couple stayed together when they came to an agreement and left the cult at the same time.

There was a family that I will change the name to Kitchen. The Kitchen family had lived in Louisiana before that congregation was shut down and all its members ordered to relocate. The Kitchen family moved to California. They had a fairly large family and made the transition from a rural country setting to right in the heart of a large city life.

Mother Kitchen after a few years had a longing to go back home for a visit with her friends and relatives. Month after month Mr. Kitchen would say no, or later, or sometime. Years went by and Mrs. Kitchen got an idea. She secretly packed suitcases for a week's vacation. One morning right after Mr. Kitchen left for work she left a note for him, took the children and drove off for Louisiana.

Surprise! When she got to her destination, her husband was already there waiting for her. He had taken a plane and beat her there. He was angry but acted like it was going to be alright. However, when she woke up in the morning, she found herself abandoned. Mr. Kitchen had taken the van, the children, all her money, credit cards, driver's license, actually her entire purse. She was left with nothing to make the trip back to California. She was given the trauma of trying to figure out how that is possible.

Hearing that, and what I experienced the eight years that I was with them, I can see the finger prints of the master mind, Danny Layne, behind all of this. Even if her relatives gave her the money, I vicariously cringe and shudder at the worst that is still to come... the shunning from the cult members. The only way back in is to cry long and hard at the altar, followed by publicly apologizing in front of the entire congregation. Fear control and mind control are two strong factors to keep their group and practices together. Danny is the master mind behind it.

There was a mother that I know that told me that she had problems with the cult's teaching on discipline too. She felt it was way too abusive, or that she was just too timid for it. This struggle was related to Danny. He took it upon himself to train her on how to be more forceful in training children for the Lord. One day she received an order from Danny to come quickly for some training in how to discipline. When she got there she was ushered into his office which is in California. What she experienced, she told me that she will never forget. Besides herself, and Danny, there was a teenage boy of one of the mothers within that cult. The boy had violated some rule of their probably illegal and private school, and was sentenced to get his discipline in Danny's office.

First Danny explained what happened and then elaborated on how serious the crime was. He started strutting around the office like he was devil possessed. He was swinging this leather strap around as if this whole training must begin with a great fear instilled into the boy. With swiftness Danny would whip the leather strap unto the table to cause tremendous fear. If the boy had all this evil and hellish behavior inside of him when he got to the office, Danny evidently was doing a fine job at scaring the hell right out of him before their confrontation was over!

This mother told me that this so called lesson was the most violent discipline session she had ever witnessed in her life. Danny was acting like a monster in there and anything but what she would perceive a Christian would act like. That experience changed her mind about this pious and godly image that Danny was portraying; it was totally the opposite. He was an actor that had deceived for himself a following. If only the actions like this incident could be recorded on video, that man would be behind bars, and rightfully so. He has caused a lot of heartache and trauma in a lot of people's lives.

A different mother had a daughter that refused to follow the ways of this cult. The daughter was probably in her late teenage years at the time and could not be thrown out of the house yet. Danny counseled the mother seriously but yet kind of as a joke that she should go into her daughter's bedroom at night when she is sleeping, and then beat her with a 2x4! Oh yes, that man has a very hateful and violent spirit.

One example of fabricated doctrine with no Bible verses to support it is the teaching by Danny on his ideas on proper greetings and the counter response. He basically started a self-made doctrine out of this issue. I remember vividly his teaching about how the only proper salutation in greeting someone of their group is to say, "Praise the Lord!" Saying, "Hi" or "Good Morning", is not the Saintly way to greet each other. It became mandatory to say, "Praise the Lord" every time we met another one of our church (cult) members.

That was bizarre enough but the weirdness became worse. For the person that gets addressed with, "Praise the Lord", they can only give one response. They cannot say, "Yes, praise the Lord" in return, or anything else besides, "Yes, Amen!" That is the only response acceptable and it was mandatory, unless you didn't fit in and wanted them to boot you out. Where is the scripture for that? It is nothing more than man-made rules to embalm the non-thinkers into following the cult the next time they come up with something even stranger and non-Biblical. Their minds become so warped that if they accidentally just said, "Hi" instead of "Praise the Lord", they would feel convicted and "back-slidden". Good chances are that at the very next service, they will go to the altar to repent for violating the churches rules which are ultimately God's rules that they broke.

There was another meeting that Danny preached at. He stated that it is not Saintly to give added names to people and he was basically directing it to our children. What he was referring to was that we don't call one of our children, "My rosebud", "My precious", or "My little tiger", or whatever you call them. He elaborated on that for quite a while on how wrong and un-saintly that would be for us to use other nicknames like that.

Unfortunately, I didn't have a response at that moment even though his comments troubled me. Maybe it was best that I didn't have the thought I got after wards, because if I had, he would have applied pressure much quicker at getting rid of me. What was my idea and notion that I thought of on a later day? My thought became this and I will state it sarcastically. It is NOT the way I see it.

"It is a wonderful blessing to follow this man, Danny Layne that is so intelligent and even smarter than Jesus." Even Jesus didn't know the truth about calling people names and that he was un-saintly. He called two of his disciples, "Sons of thunder", and another one "the stone." He called the Scribes and Pharisees a bunch of things like "whitened sepulchres full of dead mens bones" and other names. He called one of the Roman rulers a fox.

Jesus definitely violated Danny's great wisdom and knowledge. Considering all these little issues like this one, proves that within that group there are a lot of errors. Once you find several errors, consider that there are many more that you have not discovered. With those errors in mind, a person has to see that it is NOT God's Church reaching down to man or us. In reality, it is an arrogant man that has deceived several people to follow him, trying to reach up to God, but trying to convince others that they are the messengers from the throne of God, even though they have had very little contact with God. If they did have close contact with God, why could they never reach him when one of their members or children are facing death? If they have a life threatening illness, they die! They will quickly defend their Divine Healing practice by pointing out several people that were healed from the common cold, a headache, or something like that. Would you call a gradual disappearance of a headache, a sign of divine healing power and that they had a close connection with God to be able to get that?

There are several double standards in their midst. If they hear or see something done foolishly by another church, they preach about it from the pulpit. However, if one of their choice members does something foolish, they cover it up or laugh about it. I heard they made a joke about the following when I tried making an issue out of it.

Patrick Jr. was right around twenty years of age. He decided to make my children laugh and so he put shaving cream on his face

147

making it look like he had a white beard. Then he took some of his own siblings plus some of my children for a ride around the city of Kenosha. They would go through a drive through at a few fast food restaurants. Once in front of the window, he would tell them that he lost his reindeer somewhere and asked them if they had seen them anywhere. He said one of them answers to the name of Rudolph. The children laughed at this unusual circumstance. They don't believe in Christmas and say it is a pagan holiday. Santa Claus is condemned highly. Then why all this behavior from someone brought up with those beliefs?

When I was excommunicated and shunned, I wrote a letter to their ministry asking them why this double standard? Why do I get excommunicated because I wanted to spend one Sunday with my grieving family two months after Mom died, but then nothing gets done about a Santa Claus impersonation done in public? The cult made fun of my letter. A witness told me that a minister went up to Patrick Jr. and asked him if he was going to get any Christmas presents from him this year? Why this double standard? If "your" church would have been spotted doing that, we would have heard sermons on what "Babylon" is doing out there. "Thank God we have been pulled out of Babylon", they would say.

Intimidation

That group is proficient at intimidation. During one of my court trials, the cult scheduled a week-long series of services for their congregation. The court date was on one of the mid-week days of their meeting.

As I came into the courthouse, I noticed several cult members in the hallways fully clothed in their long standard black and white clothing. Once I walked into the courtroom, up front in the martyrdom section of the arena, I sat down curious at who else was in the court room. Even though fearful, I turned around for just a couple of seconds. Wow! The place seemed to be invaded with those black and white penguins! There must have been twenty or more of these mentally deranged or demented individuals. Danny, the "top dog", was in the front row!

Was this some kind of collusion between them along with the

judge, and against me? Seeing that many cult members displaying their support against you, makes the effects of mental hypothermia I mentioned in the first chapter, take its course. My heart instantly started making cartwheels inside of me, threatening to jump right out of my mouth. That cult knows how to create fear.

My mind flashed back to Elmer, Ontario. One family of that congregation had gotten investigated by a child protection agency for claims of child abuse. The family admitted that they disciplined according to the cult teaching. Because of this warped philosophy on "spanking", the children were taken from this family. The rest of the Ontario mothers with children fled to Ohio and Indiana. The fugitive families were housed by the "Saints" that lived in the United States. After they had fled, the family that had their children removed from them received a court date for the accusations.

It was within the same week or two that the baby died in California. Danny stressed that every available "Saint" that can possibly make the trip to Ontario, should go there for that court date. I remember going with my family to show support. The entire cult met first at their church building in the morning for prayer. The ministry made some announcements of what to do and what not to do.

"Do not talk to any strangers! Any one of them could be reporters. Even if you don't see a camera or a notepad, it does not mean that they are not a reporter. If you do not obey this order, you will be in trouble with the ministry. If any other member spots a different member talking to a stranger, please notify the ministry."

Then the long convoy began to the next major city where the County courthouse was. Once within the city limits we followed the car in front of us unto a field which was now used as a parking lot. As we were locking up our van to walk to the courthouse, an informant told us to hide all of our spanking sticks. "Don't bring any with you, and don't leave them in open view inside your vehicle. Hide them under the seats or wherever," they warned us.

It was several blocks to the court house. Once there, we were ordered to form a tight group on the courthouse lawn. Our church song books were distributed among us and we began to sing. Song after song was sung while the court case was in session. If the Judge would have looked out of the window, he would have seen the penguin crowd of maybe over two or three hundred. I can't estimate quantity of people in a large crowd very well so I might be off on numbers. However, the singing could be heard in the courtroom I was told. It was all a ploy to intimidate the Judge in seeing or hearing the multitude of people outside that would oppose him if he ruled contrary to our beliefs.

Back in Kenosha, Wisconsin, the intimidation continued. I made it through the court hearing and escaped with at least my life out of the arena when it was finished. However, I already suspected and dreaded Saturday when I am supposed to pick up my children for that day.

That day came and my two oldest boys were with me. We drove the long way around their church building and looked down the street toward them. We saw people already outside. We decided then to sneak in from the East side in hopes to pick up the children from the back, and then quickly get out of there without much confrontation. As we parked we knew our plan would not work. Danny Layne was already there heading for the church house where my family lived. He noticed us and told us that my children are in the front of the church building, and that we will need to go there to pick them up.

We had no other option other than going around to the front. We did not even get to the front yet and we already saw the large crowd. As we rounded the corner, it seemed like we were confronted by over a hundred people! They all looked so sorrowful about us and our spiritual condition. Several members came up to us and made comments. "We are praying for you all," some said. "We liked you better the other way," more of them stated. "We will pray that you will all get saved."

The front steps were filled with cult members looking down at us as if we were some kind of freak show. I looked around and couldn't see my children. It seemed like some kind of hostage scene or showdown. Suddenly as if Moses was parting the Red

Sea, the cult members started to move to make a corridor so that there was a small passage way to the front door. Mercy! Are they expecting us to enter through that two foot passage?

Fortunately instead though, I saw my children coming through that narrow opening as if the cult was giving birth to them. We just had to deal with a few more cutting remarks about our lost condition as we headed for the van. As soon as we had loaded every one of my children, we were released from this lesson on how to intimidate and shun ex-cult members. They sure relish in that kind of behavior!

Usually when a member breaks the cult's rules, they get plenty of attention. I have seen, sometimes three or four pastors interrogating just one single misfit or victim. The unfortunate victim usually comes out of the arena with tear stained eyes. A good CoGR ministry motto could be, "There we were, two against a thousand... the toughest two we ever fought!" Intimidation by numbers is a very much used tactic of theirs.

CHAPTER 8

CLOSURE OF OUR FIRST CONGREGATION

At one camp meeting Danny Layne called the entire Spooner congregation into a meeting. He pulled the plug on us and everyone was ordered to relocate to one of their other established congregations. Our pastor moved on to California, but later left the church completely.

Shereen became unhappy living in northern Wisconsin and began nagging me on a daily basis to move to Kenosha to be closer to the Saints, as the members of CoGR called themselves, preaching that all others are "The Ain'ts." I was apprehensive. Something in my gut told me that it was not a good idea to move to Southeastern Wisconsin to be closer to that congregation. I became weary of Shereen's nagging though.

I made many excuses as to why we could not move to Kenosha. Our home, the one I had built with my own hands, was here in Spooner. My work was here, even though it had slowed down because the winter was approaching. Until the ground freezes hard, it usually slows down in the late fall.

With each excuse that I had, the church had a solution. We were offered a home in Kenosha, rent free. The church began to solicit work for me as a tree cutter. I had only worked for others before and here they were offering me the opportunity to work for myself. And to top it all off, Pat O'Shea offered his teenage sons as free labor until I became established. I sold the animals and moved to Kenosha.

Within the first few months the Ralph Salz's death occurred. Listening to Pat lie I knew I had made a mistake of moving there. I told Shereen that I would love to move back to Spooner.

"There is nothing up there," she said. "There is no

congregation. I am not going to be isolated. Why do you want to move back up north?"

"I have no place to park my equipment down here in Kenosha. Up north I can park it in my yard." I responded.

"Life is more than parking equipment, you need to consider our souls," she argues back.

"I still would like to go back to Spooner," I tried to explain to her.

In defiance she stated, "Well, I'm not going!"

I knew then my marriage was hanging on a fragile thread. No more will she move where ever I desire to go. If I desire to move back to Spooner, I have to move by myself. What have I done?

Almanac Project

The cult preached that they were the only right group. All other churches and people were either Babylon or the unsaved. I did not agree with that doctrine. A person that believes that everyone who claims to be saved will be in Heaven has too broad a perspective. Every person that believes that only their church will go to heaven has too narrow of a perspective. The Bible says, that from every tongue, every country, or every tribe, individuals will be redeemed to God. This cult's perspective of who is going to make heaven is too small.

I bought an Almanac and did a little project. I wrote down the populations of every country listed. I then asked how many "Saints," who according to the CoGR are the only people who will make it to heaven, are located in each of these countries. Outside of the US, Canada, Mexico, Germany, one country in Africa, and possibly a person or two in the Philippines, the number is ZERO! According to the seventh chapter of the book of Revelation, there would be people from "all nations and tribes and people and tongues."

I continued with my project, taking an eye dropper and counting out how many drops filled a teaspoon and calculated from there the number of drops that would be in a gallon. If each drop represents one thousand people, the population of the world today would fill more than fifty 55-gallon drums. Imagine those drums filled with dirty black oil. This represents the number of people who, according to the CoGR, are going to hell. Now compare three drops of clean water right beside ALL of the oil, and you have the example of three thousand chosen "Saints", (them), who will make it into Heaven. At the time the cult had only about three thousand members which represents the three drops of pure water! Having this visual representation, painted a clear picture for me as to the ridiculousness of the CoGR's claim.

Upon presenting my pictured project with all the drawing of barrels filled with black oil, did not bring me much praise from their pastors. Pat basically told me that I am in a dire and serious spiritual condition.

Hunting and Fishing

Some people can't grasp the seriousness of the danger or threat of this group. I vividly remember the sermons on recruiting others as one of their main focuses. They would actually use the verse Jeremiah 16:16, where it said that the Lord will send forth hunters and fishers to gather all of God's people.

It was a common practice or experience to hear the announcement that the following Wednesday evening or Sunday evening, our entire congregation will attend a different church, (possibly yours) to just "fellowship" with that group of people, but we all referred it as going fishing. Most people get excited if they would receive fifty, or a hundred or more "visitors" at one of their services. Seeing every seat fill up in the sanctuary with visitors is usually an exciting and remembered service. The normal tendency for people when they get visitors is to make them feel welcome.

However, while they are nice to these CoGR's visitors, they don't realize what is going on right under their nose undetected. These CoGR members are hunting and fishing for serious and discontented individuals amongst "your" congregation. They discreetly try to get names and addresses of these possible recruits and future CoGR members.

A few times I witnessed the fishing of this cult not to be very discreet. Once, several cult members in Kenosha took anti-Catholic tracts which were disguised as "commands of Mary". The cult passed them out at a Catholic Church parking lot while the Catholic members were heading for their mass. It wasn't until after they took the tract and went inside their large church, that they realized the anti-Catholic contents. After they were inside the building scanning the catholic bashing contents, they got mad. Evidently, somebody came out and ordered them away from their property. I heard the cult members bragging at how many tracts they had distributed before they were ordered to leave. They laughed about how eager the Catholics were at taking something to do with Mary. I am happy I was not part of that incident.

Another time when I was involved though, we were at a Wal-Mart in Kenosha. There was quite a disturbance when one of our cult members insisted on giving an irate customer a tract. The Wal-Mart customer refused to take the tract and yet Johnny kept pressuring him into accepting the tract. The majority of us just kept on singing our church songs, while this commotion was taking place in front of our eyes. Johnny kept insisting for the angry person to take the tract telling him it could save his soul, while the irate person yelled back, "Save your own soul!" It turned into a shouting match until the customer was so mad that he went back into the store with an angered motive. Within minutes, the manager came out and ordered all of us to leave.

The church visiting is usually a lot more peaceful and deceptive. It also proved to be more affective. Once the CoGR members are back in their own turf, they excitedly exchange the notes and names of whoever they found. While our pastor sidetracks their pastor, it was our duty to get names and addresses.

All the interesting happenings get shared with the group. Then mysteriously those restless souls of your congregation will in a few weeks get a Gospel Trumpet paper sent to them. By then they will not consider why they received it, and that it derived directly from giving their name indiscreetly or laxly to the visitors. If they truly are discontent with your church, they will read the paper which will slide them down this slope to their inevitable doom.

What I mean by that is that there are few options of escape. If they have a family, it is very likely that that family will be ripped apart in the next few years. Many, and I stress many, marriages have been destroyed by this cult. My marriage is only one of the many that was destroyed. I know of many more marriages that one or the other of the spouses were told to leave their mate for the saving of their soul. The Bible story of Ananias and Sapphira (Acts 5) will be thrust into their mind. "Will you lose your soul because of your spouse that is hindering you from following the One, True Church?" "You will need to leave them temporarily", they will say.

Another inevitable doom is that your mind is being set up for the worst psychological roller coaster in your life. You can read chapter ten to just get a tiny idea what I am talking about. Almost all ex-members that get shunned or kicked out of this cult do not make it. What I mean is that sure physically they move on but they leave mentally and spiritually in such an attitude that they hate God or anything religious in nature. I have known some to turn to drugs and alcohol just to prove that they no longer are CoGR. No matter how long the person is physically out of the cult, I have not reached the time limit yet of when the cult gets removed out of the victim mentally. Maybe it will be never, or at death.

Lawsuit over Washington Campground

I found it ironic the double standard that the cult has when dealing with lawsuits. If an ex-member would file a lawsuit against the cult for mental or emotional damages, they would point out to their congregation at how far this person has fallen from the teachings of Christ. However, few people know what happened in the State of Washington.

There used to be one of their congregations in Nooksack, Washington. Because Danny Layne had given a few dollars toward the original purchase of the church grounds, and because it was considered Church Of God Restoration property, Danny determined that it was his property. When almost the entire congregation "woke up" to the understanding that they were following a man, Danny Layne, instead of God and his principles, they broke away from the cult. That breaking away, needed to be done in a paper documentation, much more than just verbally.

Several leaders of the cult along with Danny instantly filed a lawsuit against the Nooksack congregation. They tried suing the camp and church grounds away from them, even though the local members had paid nearly the entire purchase price themselves. If the cult would have won the lawsuit, they simply would have sold the grounds to get the money value of it. Where was the Christian outlook of not suing someone then? The cult must have reasoned that it was not suing a "Brother", so therefore it was permissible.

The outcome was a great victory for the local members. The Judge saw through Danny Layne's greed and motive, and ruled in favor for the local congregation. If you want to see the Judge's decision statement, read it at my friend's website that I already mentioned- www.churchofgodrestorationexposed.us

CHAPTER 9
THE BEGINNING OF THE END

A lesson that I've learned from my experiences is that you can't force someone to love you. You only have 50% of the control in your marriage. If your spouse is 100% against you, your marriage is over. The only way that Shereen would have stayed with me, was if I would have worshiped the CoGR more than God, the way she did. They preach to the spouse who wants to be part of their church that they must choose between God and their marriage. "Will you be like Ananias and Sapphira and lose your lives, because together they lied against the Holy Spirit and the Church?"

I could not stay within the group that I was beginning to think of as a cult. By the order and advice of the ministry of the Church of God Restoration, Shereen was already gone emotionally, and soon to be physically also.

I offer this time line as a chain of events, starting from when I first became disillusioned by the Church of God Restoration.

When we moved to Kenosha, Wisconsin, Shereen and I lived with our children on the upper level of the assistant pastor's house. Living below, with the assistant pastor, was Ralph Salz. I already wrote about how he died and everything that took place around that event. Shereen already had made it very clear that she was not leaving Kenosha and definitely NOT this cult. I had witnessed how Pat and Danny connived together with this lie of omission and deceit. I desired to leave then, but Shereen's defiance hindered me. Instead of walking away from the cult which meant also walking away from my family, I started to try to find some good in this group even though I saw nasty traits within this system.

I wish I would have smelled the rat poison earlier before I moved to Kenosha. Next time you buy rat poison, please look at the ingredients. You will find about 99.9% good corn and oats as the main ingredient. That should be a hearty meal, right? The problem is that to about one part poison, there is a thousand parts good things that are not poisonous. That is not very much poison, is it? It does seem innocent and insignificant. It is enough to kill!

The same goes for this cult. Go pay them a visit, and if they don't tell you all their rules, you might even enjoy their service or of being in their company. Just watch out for the hidden poisons that could lure you into your doom. The worst is if your children get doomed into this, which have no choice of where their parents want them to attend worship.

This group does have a lot of "Good corn and oats." If you are spiritually heading toward them they will give of their time and money to please you any which way they can. However, if you sense a little trace of poison and desire to leave, they become the most hostile and vicious people I have ever met, and yet they call themselves Christians at that! I just wish I would have known the contents of this book or at least about their rules back in the mid-1990's.

After this incident with the death of Ralph Salz, I began to question the group that I had become involved with. If they could so easily bend words to suit their purposes with the law, what else might they be wrong about?

In July of 2001, I made plans with my children, to travel to Minnesota to visit with relatives for the weekend. This would require us to miss church services on Sunday. Before we had packed up to leave, Shereen contacted Pat O'Shea, informing him of my plans. Pat O'Shea came into my house and interrogated each of the children, while ignoring me and behaving as if I wasn't even in the room. He ordered me to stay out of it.

He asked each child in turn if they really wanted to go up North, more that they wanted God. He told them that if they missed services on Sunday they could no longer consider themselves saved. He told them if they weren't in church on Sunday, that they would then be on their way to hell. For about an hour he tormented them with fear, until the children in tears promised him that they did not want to go. I decided that next time I wouldn't tell Shereen my plans.

A few months after this event, in September, I needed to head to Minnesota to fix my stump grinding equipment. My intention was to leave on Friday and be back for services on Sunday. Pat O'Shea announced that this was impossible as Saturday had been declared a mandatory church workday. After arguing with him he finally conceded that I could go, but ordered that the children would not be allowed to go with me.

Against O'Shea's wishes I packed up my five oldest children the next evening and we headed to Minnesota. I phoned Shereen as soon as I got to the interstate, and told her that we would be back for Sunday services.

Upon our return, Pat O'Shea took my children in his private room. There he interrogated my children to tears, denouncing us all and telling them that the six of us were no longer saved. Then it was my turn! After that for at least the next thirty minutes he screamed in my face, "You are lost! You are no longer a brother! Shereen is going to get the Children! You are going to be destroyed!" He told me it was impossible for me to be saved. I did not tell Shereen about my plans with the children until we had already gone, which is deception. Deception is a lie. And liars go to hell! I mentioned all of this already in the beginning of this book. At that point Shereen was ordered to sleep separate from me. I was shunned for quite some time after that. They treated me as if I was Anthrax.

As part of their daily attire, the men of the CoGR wear a black vest over a long-sleeved button down shirt and a t-shirt beneath that. I refused to wear that hot vest outside when it was ninety degrees. I was definitely breaking their dress code. My oldest boys, Randy and David, asked if they could have relief from their vests as well. I told them yes. Their mother demanded that they had to wear the vests and told me to enforce this. I did not back her up and as a result I was back in O'Shea's office, being told that if I do not support my wife's wishes, she needed to leave me.

I had several arguments with Pat O'Shea regarding watching television. I did not agree with the stance of absolute abstinence. We had stopped at a truck stop while traveling and there was live

TV footage of the clean-up of the Twin Towers following September 11, 2001. My children had not been able to see any footage of the falling towers and I allowed them to watch the crews at work moving debris and wreckage from Ground Zero. I was reprimanded for this as well.

In December of 2001, at a family Christmas party held by Shereen's family, her aunts offered me wine on several occasions and I declined. I do not have a strong conviction against alcohol. I just prefer not to drink it and had not done so in more than fifteen years. I do have a strong conviction against intoxication, and therefore have never been drunk in my life. When my daughter Suzy came to me with her little Dixie cup filled from the wrong punch bowl, I told her, "Everything the Restoration says is not entirely accurate. Drinking this is not a sin," and I swallowed the little bit of wine that was in her cup. I told her not to make the same mistake again. I will not drink it the next time. Suzy told Shereen and she in turn told Pat O'Shea.

I was called into O'Shea's office where he proceeded to yell at me once again, with his finger stabbing the air in front of me again for quite some time. "You are not saved! You need to stand up in front of the entire congregation and admit and apologize that you have sinned! I never did that which created even more tension between us.

On a Sunday morning, Shereen was having an argument with Randy and David. She told the boys that I wasn't saved because I refused to repent over that one swallow of wine. Their response was that I was concerned with waste and drank the little bit of wine rather than waste it down the drain. She argued that I hadn't taken that into consideration. When the boys told her she was lying, that she couldn't know what another was thinking, Shereen immediately told Pat O'Shea.

Back to O'Shea's office again, right after Sunday morning church service. I was like a child waiting to be dealt a punishment by the school principal, along with my two boys, and Shereen present also. My boys were reproved for saying that Shereen was a liar. Then I was forcefully addressed.

161

"Tell your boys to say that their mother is not lying," O'Shea said to me.

"But that's exactly why I drank the wine," I responded.

O'Shea flew into a rage.

"I have tried to keep this marriage together, but it is over!" he yelled. "Someone else had told me to break your marriage up a long time ago, but I thought there was hope. I now know that I was wrong."

The person that wanted it broke up could only be Danny Layne. Who else could it be?

He commanded Shereen to leave me right then. She left us immediately to go to his place. I then argued with him for three hours, trying desperately to salvage my marriage. He allowed Shereen to return home with me that evening, but we were on shaky ground. She still refused to display affection toward me. It is all part of their shunning tactics.

After only a few short days, Shereen verbally attacked me again.

"You need to repent! You need to get saved!" she said. I told her that I didn't believe in everything that the CoGR preached and practiced. She ran for the phone.

"Please don't call him," I said. "I don't want to talk to him."

I went upstairs to our room. Within five minutes Pat O'Shea was knocking at our door. I heard Shereen letting him in.

"Where is Bernie?" He asked.

"Upstairs", I heard her respond. "He doesn't want to see you."

"Well, I guess then I will go see him," he responded and he came upstairs uninvited and unwanted into my bedroom.

We argued and he did not leave until well after midnight. He instructed Shereen to sleep separately from me until I submitted to the teachings of the church. This went on for one week until I made an appeal to Danny Layne to have it stopped. She returned to our bed, but remained on her side. At the time in 2002, there were six marriages within the Kenosha congregation, and a few single people. Of the six, three of them were either separated or divorced, because of this cult. Mine was one of those three.

Suddenly my mom died of cardiac arrest in January of 2002. I brought my family to Minnesota so I could help my Dad bury her. I spoke with my Dad in German, about what a good wife he had. Shereen, misunderstanding the German, picked a fight with me after we got back to Kenosha, accusing me that I said that I had a bad wife. I explained to her that I had only said that she was not as passive as my Mom had been. That too was more fuel for Pat O'Shea to reprove me.

In March of that same year, Randy and David were forced to attend a camp meeting in California against both my wishes and their own. Pat O'Shea just ordered my family to go and leave me behind to work. The total control was taken away from me, Pat made all the decisions. If I resisted, Shereen would leave that moment.

Then for Easter, my siblings planned to get together in memory of our Mom. I asked my children if they would like to attend this occasion and they respond with resounding yes. Shereen argued that we couldn't go.

"We will miss church," she stated.

"You've just been gone to a camp meeting for nine days in California, and I can't take the children for one day? In memory of mom? I asked.

"That's a stupid reason to miss church," she answered.

I told her that I had about two hours of work to do and I would like an answer when I returned. I didn't know that this would be the last time I would ever hug or kiss her. When I came home at three-thirty Shereen and the younger children were gone. She wouldn't answer her cell phone which I was paying for. I checked the O'Shea house and it looked deserted. The drapes were closed tight and it was dark. No one answered the door. I didn't see them for the next thirty five days.

Those next thirty-five days was the time it took for the courts to establish our first hearing which allowed me placement. Before that time, she hid my children from me. I have witnessed the cult take individuals in a situation like this, and ship them across the country to another cult member of another state. There was a forbidden secret romance going on in Kenosha. The pastor's son and the assistant's pastor's daughter were secretly passing notes back and forth to each other. It was found out and the congregation had a problem on their hands. One of the solutions recommended, was that the O'Shea family would move to the congregation in Louisiana, where a pastor was needed. The Louisiana's pastor was taken out of that position because of some "sin".

When that option didn't work out, the cult simply shipped the daughter to California, to live with a family there. The cult does those things to "protect" their members from violating any rules, or to "protect" members from the foes of the cult. My website is linked to www.rickross.com . Rick Ross is a investigator into cults, and posts his findings on his site. If you check out the newspaper articles in his CoGR section, you can read how all the women and children fled Canada, and hid out amongst the cult families living in Indiana and Ohio. Why? To "protect" the members from the "foes", which were the Child Protection Agency this time. Read the details in approximately thirty articles on that website.

When Randy, David and I returned home after the two day trip to Minnesota, Shereen and the children were still gone. The messages on the answering machine had been checked, so she had stopped in at some point. I contacted the police department to see what my rights were. I had to file a missing family report.
That night two detectives stopped by the house to tell me that my family was staying at the O'Shea's. They couldn't make them come home. I would need an attorney.

On April 2, 2002, I called O'Shea's house. The son, Patrick, Jr, told me I needed to talk to the assistant pastor and hung up. I contacted James the assistant pastor.

"You tried to miss a church service without permission," he told me. "You won't see your family again until you get some serious spiritual help."

A few days later I saw an attorney, Ward, who told me that I MUST get a divorce if I wanted to see my children again.

I told him I didn't want a divorce. I disputed quite a while with him. He told me there was nothing else that he or anyone else could do if I didn't file for a divorce. Unless I signed the papers I would not be able to see my children. Out of ignorance, I signed the papers with him. After the divorce was final, I found out from a different attorney that a divorce was not the only way, I could have filed for just Child Placement which would have been much cheaper. That is exactly what I wanted. Attorney Ward had lied to me.

I called the O'Shea's house and left a message on their answering machine stating that I will call the police for the abuse my boys withstood at O'Shea's hands, if Shereen didn't call me. She called back on the speaker phone, with the congregation whispering responses in the background.

I had Randy and David living with me, while Shereen had the five youngest children with her at the O'Shea's. We were living in the rental house that Shereen and I lived in after moving from the assistant pastor's house. In the house were some unwanted visitors: cockroaches!

On several occasions I implored Shereen to please take care of the problem with store bought insect bombs. She refused, listing all the extra work it would create for her: washing all the linens and clothing, clearing all of the cabinets, washing all of the dishes in the house and so forth. The fumigation was never done and we lived for about two years with the roaches.

After Shereen left in March, she called the Health Department immediately, reporting that the house was not fit for the boys to be living there because of the cockroaches and filth. The morning that the woman from the Health Department came, I was on my way out the door. She told me why she was there and I began to explain the entire situation to her. I talked about the contents of this book concerning this cult.

She seemed to understand that Shereen was playing dirty, and assured me that she was not there to report an untidy bachelor pad. She just needed to make sure it wasn't in need of condemning. She came into the house, took note of a few dirty dishes, the unwashed floors and the rugs were in need of vacuuming. She wished me well and was on her way. She was back within a week. Shereen had called again insisting that the house be re-inspected, that it was infested with cockroaches, the same roaches that she had lived with for two years. Again the woman had a look around and left. The Human services can only come out twice for the same complaint. Without extra evidence after that, it becomes an invasion of privacy to the people that get checked on, and therefore restricted.

That rule can go both ways. If I know that children are getting abused in this system, I can get that service to investigate only twice. After that, the agency and I are restricted from invading their privacy. Unless I have more proof, the parents can beat the child black and blue after that without getting investigated.

CHAPTER 10

THE CAPTIVITY RELEASE OF THE MIND AND SOUL

The entire human being of body, mind, soul, and spirit becomes a hostage of the cult after a while. Every thought and action done becomes the captivity and also doom of the entire being. When a confrontation arises and a one time member gets excommunicated in this cult, the separate identities of a human, which I have mentioned, must under-go a savage and brutal attack.

The body can be pitched out of their midst any moment. However, the thoughts, mind, spirit and soul, becomes the battleground that almost every victim of this cult loses. Hearing over, and over again, all the false teachings for several years, just doesn't vanish the moment the body leaves. Therefore, the body gets torn from the spiritual and thought side of the entire being, causing such torment in the mind that it is difficult to explain. It is far worse than being abandoned by a spouse or parent, because being excommunicated is that, plus the mental torment.

Fears of being lost, haunts the mind. Have I actually left the One,True Church? If all other churches are sin and Babylon, what is the use of even trying to go to a different church? For years you sat listening how to detect all the sins that they mentioned by their rules. As soon as you start seeking another place to fellowship, the new place is filled with all the things that were condemned.

One day the mind wants to believe it is alright to fellowship with some other believers, but the heart condemns the people. The next moment the heart wants to overlook the visual programed spiritual filth, and look at the heartfelt things, but then the mind refuses this nonsense of compromise. The war rages furiously in the unseen realm and wearies the entire demeanor or being.

Most ex-members fall by the wayside quickly not knowing

what or how to think. Where can a person get professional help when they were programmed that the very help you need is Babylon too? If I suspected you to be a con, right away I would be on guard to keep you from getting to me, even if you were sincerely trying to help me.

A picture of this is like getting pushed over a cliff by someone you thought was your friend. It might have even been your parents, child or spouse. By the slightest bit of fate you caught a small branch going down. Hanging there you venture to look down and see nothing but darkness since the depth is so great. Horror grips you as you realize your predicament. You can call out to your "friend", but what kind of a friend would push you over in the first place? A person comes by and offers to help, but they have a red shirt on. You were programmed that people with red clothing are bad people. Maybe they wear a tie or some jewelry so you condemn them too. You are scared of them because your mind was falsely programmed, but your heart wants to secure this hope. The battle rages trying to figure everything out. Nothing makes sense. Most people give up and let go. It is not instant death because the body is still alive. Only the mind and the spirit let go. Is there any hope? Is there any way a person can get back on top? How could a person ever walk into another church or congregation and be able to trust the minister that has all these taught corruptions right in his midst. Either he has a defiant congregation, or he is just a hireling that is not preaching the full truth.

I will inform you of what helped me. A person must become a free thinker again. The cult trained their victims to use a magnifying glass to find the sin in other people. They made up their own version of sin as they went along. You must fight fire with fire. Through my battles with the cult and their ministry, I already had doubts of their integrity or authenticity. Use the magnifying glass on them for a change. Look and search for their contradictions. Once you find it, challenge your mind to really discern the true meaning of what you found. That is just the key that will help unlock the door. You must still unlock and push, don't give up! Let me explain.

I already mentioned the death of Ralph Salz. I noticed how the pastor lied. Remember also about the response of the question given in the courtroom that "we didn't know how sick the child was." I will proceed at telling you of dishonesty within this group. If they are dishonest in these areas, could they have also been dishonest by giving a false view of what is required to make heaven, or who it is that is considered Babylon? I will give more examples.

To finish the story that I left you hanging with in the last chapter, it was a great confirmation to me, that I DIDN'T leave (got kicked out) the One, True Church. Let me finish it.

My placement with my other five children was on Saturday and today is Thursday. I called Shereen up and asked if I could alter the time schedule slightly. She "un-Christ-like" snaps back, "No!"

Oshkosh, Wisconsin is about three hours from Kenosha. The world famous air show was taking place this week. The exhibits take place all day long. However the air show of stunt flying starts at five o'clock, and last about two hours until about seven. If I left the air show after it finished, I would get the children back to Kenosha at about ten o'clock at night. The problem was that my placement is from 8 am to 8 pm. In order to abide by those rules I would need to leave for home just as the show begins.

I offered to compromise and pick up the children two hours later than usual so they could stay two hours later than usual, so they could watch the show. She said, "No!" I hand the phone to my two sons with me that want to go to the show too. They plead with their mommy about changing times. Why should she be so unreasonable? She was pushed by the cult. After much begging, she did make a counter deal. She would come to my house the next day to get some stuff that she left when she abandoned our two boys and me. We set the time, I think it was about 4 pm.

The next day which was Friday, the three of us rushed home to be prepared when Shereen would get there. Yesterday she had told me that she could bring a friend for protection. Wow! We were married seventeen years and I never abused her, but now she needs protection from me?

This is where the story continues that was left unfinished, at the end of the last chapter. I was going to make sure that the house was not in a greater mess than how she had kept it for the seventeen years that we were married. Quick, let us get the few dishes washed or at least hide them. Oops, too late! There is the knock at the door. Oh well, this will have to do.

We stepped outside to see our visitors. There is Shereen with her "protection friend." The friend definitely is not part of this cult. Shereen is standing there in the usual dress down to her ankles, long sleeves, and bottomed up to her neck and all her hair put up in a bun on top of her head. On the contrast, this other woman was very loose in modesty. If I remember correctly, she had on shorts and kind of like a halter top, which exposed a lot of skin. The contrast was not much different than a fish and a squirrel being friends.

"Are you ready to let me get my stuff?" she begins.

"What do you want, I will get it for you," I answer.

"No, I am getting the stuff because I don't remember it all," she insists.

We were ordered by the courts that I should not set foot in her dwelling, and that she should not step into mine. But now she is demanding to step into my house to get the stuff. What stuff? She doesn't even know.

"I would rather not have you come into my house," I counter respond.

"Well then, OK, you can't get the children tomorrow beyond eight o'clock then," was her response.

"OK, you can come in then," I reluctantly answered.

"This is Tiffany. Can she come in the house with me?

"No!" Even though this woman does not look anything like the cult, I did not need more people than necessary in my house invading my privacy. I don't know who she is. She is definitely not dressed like a professional woman.

"Well, can Randy and David stay outside here then too?" Shereen objects.

"What do you mean? They live here!"

"Where are they going to be?" she asks.

"They can remain in the kitchen," I assure her.

"Well, can Tiffany remain in the kitchen also?" was her request.

I was tired of this negotiating, and besides, what harm can this loose dressed woman do? So I conceded to let them in.

Once inside, the first room is the kitchen which leads into the living room. Tiffany entered but stood right by the entrance door. Randy and David stood to one side of the room where they could watch everyone. I was already in the entry of the living room. Shereen was just in front of me but still in the kitchen. She had her back towards me facing Tiffany. The stage was set.

The boys told me that Shereen then winked at Tiffany, ready to spring the trap upon me. She then reached into her purse and pulled out a disposable camera! Oh no! My mind raced over all the things she could do with that camera. She could find a cockroach and capture the proof. Or she could focus the camera in on the biggest mess that she could find. She had left us with the spare bedroom stacked with her junk, clear to the ceiling in a few places. There was just one narrow trail that she had left, so that she could get to the closet, which was piled full also. This means trouble! She will take the pictures so she can send the Health department after me again.

I demanded, "No pictures!"

"Yes, I can take pictures," she said in defiance.

She raises the camera to her face and aims at my table cluttered with papers for this legal battle and my cult research! It is a mess, but what does that mess have to do with her getting her stuff?

"No pictures", I requested one more time, but she proceeded to bring the camera up.

What could I do? I needed to stop her or else my two boys will be taken from me. I will try to snatch the camera from out of her hands. She was ready, so I believe it was all preplanned. As I attempted to grab the camera, she immediately saw my hand coming, and so she quickly lowered the camera and started screaming. Behind me at the same moment, Tiffany started yelling at me too, "Get your hands off of her!"

I turned around and she already had dialed 911, and immediately started talking to the police. I didn't have my hands on her. I turned back and Shereen was raising the camera up to her face and shoulder area, and then rapidly lowering it back down to her knees area, back and forth very quickly, screaming the entire time like a stuck pig.

"I can take pictures, this was my house too. This is my property in this house too!" she screamed.

There were more things that she screamed, but I don't remember what else she said. I was just stunned to see a woman that I had been married to for almost seventeen years act like I was torturing her. I knew I couldn't touch her.

"Yes, there is a fight going on here", or something along those lines Tiffany told the police. "The address is ....", Tiffany begins uncertainly, and Shereen yells over her shoulder the correct address, which Tiffany then repeats. During the entire phone call, Shereen did not quit screaming. She still had the camera, and I knew that I couldn't get it, so I asked Randy to get it from her. He had just turned sixteen that month, and was capable of grabbing the camera from his mother who was trying to get him back under the abuse and authority of the cult. Shereen didn't quit screaming until the phone call was accomplished.

As soon as Randy grabbed the first camera from her, she just reached into her purse and grabbed out a second camera, and continued screaming. Seeing the next camera, Randy immediately took that camera from her too. The phone call was complete and things got quiet again.

"Get out of my house," I ordered.

Having accomplished what I believe they had planned ahead of time, they walked out of my house. I followed them out the door also, never dreaming of what would happen to me next. I thought I would just go back to work. I hadn't done anything!

The police rolled up, who I found out later was new to that occupation. He came over to me and asked me what happened, while Shereen and Tiffany stood about twenty yards away. I notice

Tiffany instructing Shereen what to do next. The police left me and walked over to them. Both of the women start telling him that I grabbed her roughly, tearing the cameras from her hands. Through the process of my violence, I supposedly hurt Shereen's wrists. She was acting out as if she was in extreme pain, holding and rubbing her wrists.

The police came back to me and told me that he could arrest me for this. I told him that I didn't touch her. The only thing that happened is that Randy grabbed the cameras from her. He mentioned that if he did arrest me, I could bail myself out for $150. If I don't have the money I would go to jail for a few days until a court hearing, probably next week sometime. I told Randy to get my hidden money.

The policeman walked back to the women, and Shereen continued complaining of how much pain she was in, rubbing her wrists the entire time. Her acting performance prompted him to walk back to me.

"Put your hands on the van," he ordered.

He was going to arrest me! Why place my hands on the vehicle, and then he must take each hand and place handcuffs on them separately, ending up with both hands behind my back? Why not avoid all of that and make it easy for him. I immediately placed my hands behind my back. Surprised, he still handcuffed me, and placed me in the back of the police car. It was summer and extremely hot in there. In my next book, "Fighting the Black Robe Conspiracy", I will elaborate what happened after that. Before I made it into jail, I was taken by ambulance to the hospital.

Several hours later I was in jail, or just the holding pen which is before you go to jail. I had to wait for my turn and for the paperwork to be completed, before my "catch and release" episode was complete. If my memory serves me right, I think it was about eleven o'clock at night before I was released. Once released, I had to walk about fifteen blocks home to where my two boys were waiting. We did not get what we wanted to accomplish.

Instead of getting the children for the later time to see the air show, we couldn't get them at all. Shereen had filled out a restraining order against me. Therefore, we weren't allowed the children at all. My two boys and I ended up going to the air show by ourselves.

Before the next weeks court hearing began, I had to face the District Attorney. He asked me how I plead. I said that I was innocent, that I didn't do anything. He then said that I might want to reconsider that under the conditions. He asked me if I knew that all 911 phone calls were recorded? Then he told me, "If there is screaming in the background I am automatically guilty, regardless what actually happened! Wow! Now I knew why Shereen screamed the entire time that Tiffany was on the phone. I then found out that Tiffany worked for a women's rights agency and knew how to pull this off, and that screaming must be on the recording. It was a set up.

Experiencing this whole thing with all the lies, I knew that I did not leave the One, True Church! This behavior and flat out lies, was not of God. She did not have Christ-like conduct, but yet she was a good member of this cult that probably told her to set me up like that. Situations like this allowed me to be convinced that this cult is a malicious and false counterfeit of Christianity. There is a lot of good "corn and oats", but the poison can kill you.

Shereen lied again in the court room that I had grabbed her and hurt her wrists which I never did. She was trying to place a year-long restraining order on me. That would mean that I would not see my children for an entire year! The accusations were that I am a violent man, which I acquired from my past when I had black market books. My past is coming out and she fears for her safety. I was ordered to explain to the judge my side of the story.

First of all, I did not grab her. I had Randy, my oldest son, take the cameras. If she got hurt it was because of the wrestling match over the cameras which she intended to frame us with. Next the so called black market books were just military books on tactics and such, and I just ordered them through the mail. As far as the past is concerned, I enjoyed making my point right there in front of everyone in the court.

"If we bring up the past to determine the present, we must

consider the following," I began saying. "I have never been drunk in my life, but she has been drunk many times in her college days!" And then I point at her as I make my point. I continued, "I have never used drugs ever in my life, but she has. So if we bring up the past, let's consider her past too".

The judge dismissed this case totally. He stated that he didn't see any threat of abuse. Shereen, Tiffany, and Sue O'Shea walked out of the court room with the facial gestures of being defeated. Someone that had been in the courtroom came to me and gave me some advice. "Watch yourself! They are trying to get you!" Does that sound like something that would have been said about Jesus? Watch him. He will frame you if you are not careful! Of course not! Therefore, I concluded that it is not "an influenced by Jesus" type of group.

Right after Shereen abandoned my two oldest boys and me, she moved in with the pastor, Pat O'Shea. I tried contacting her by her cell phone first, but she would not answer it. Next I called the O'Shea's home phone and they screened their calls by not answering my call either. However, they accidentally picked up the phone a couple of times. Once they just rudely hung it up on me. Another time Sue just stated that I must call the assistant pastor if I have anything to say, and then hung up on me.

I needed to get a hold of Shereen, so I went one morning straight to O'Shea's house. I knocked on their door and their eighteen year old son opens it, totally shocked and caught off guard seeing me stand in front of him. Disturbed he turned around to get a response of what to do from his mother. I saw her approaching less than twenty feet away within the kitchen. With indignation she gestured for her son to slam the door, which he did very swiftly. Throughout my entire life, that was the first and only time that I ever had a door slammed in my face. I had never dreamed that it would be from a pastor's house. It came from a group of people that claimed that they were the most godly and loving people on this earth!

What appalled me even more, is when I brought this up later, they made up a string of lies to cover up that action. First they mentioned that they didn't know that I wanted to talk to Shereen, even though she was living there with my other children that she was hiding from me. After I questioned the stupidity of that excuse, they switched it to that Sue O'Shea the pastor's wife, was immodest. Wow! There she was with this long night robe right down to ankles, long sleeves, and buttoned at the collar. The only "immodesty" about her, was that she still had her hair hanging down her back and not put up in a bun on top of her head. Now if she was so immodest, why was her teenage son exposed to it?

The slamming of the door, included with the lies afterward in trying to cover up their actions really helped me confirm the ungodliness of this group. Look for little confirmations like that to resolve your inward emotional conflicts. If it was of God, they would not behave in such fashion. The victim of a cult needs to consider all these incidents and reason what kind of spirit they are dealing with. It is a spirit, and discernment needs to be made if it is a "goodly" or "godly" spirit, or if it is the opposite. By the several examples that I am mentioning here, I concluded that it is not godly behavior, so therefore I only left an ungodly spirit which was and is very destructive to individuals and the family unit. Unfortunately, that evil spirit continues to torment the mind because of this fictitious hogwash or absurdity of leaving the One, True Church. Where does the mind get that concept besides from the cult that has this evil spirit in the first place? The victim must dwell on the evil of the cult, which is the origin of this spirit which tries to destroy the peace of mind. That battle continues even after their body has escaped that abusive and twisted influence.

Twisted speech

The vocabulary that the cult uses is very disturbing. In the last few paragraphs I already mentioned some of their twisted lies. They continued with other lies. Shereen didn't leave me, since she still had stuff in the house. What does taking all your stuff have to do with if you left or not? No man has ever gone to the moon then, since they still had possessions here on Earth. No person has ever gone to Heaven in that case either, because they leave it all behind. She didn't leave me, but I left her when I went to be with my grieving family. That was only a two day visit but she accused me that I abandoned her first, therefore it was permissible for her to move in with the pastor, and therefore not considered that she left me.

This loaded language or twisted speech is abundant in their midst. What you ask, the answer you hear, what you understood, what they wanted you to believe, and what they really meant, could all be different answers.

Reclusive and tight lipped

A trait that I experienced with them is how reclusive the group can be. Very few words of controversial topics get exchanged with strangers. I experienced policemen coming into the house and asking questions when the secret Kenosha romance was exposed. The assistant pastor's daughter was silently removed from Kenosha. The mother of this girl, who was not in this cult, called to speak with her. When she couldn't, she called the Kenosha police. They came and started questioning us. Since even members like us were never given all the details, I did not need to evade the truth by answering them with twisted and forked tongue speech. I didn't know where she was, but I did suspect her to be in one of the families of this cult. Later I found out that they had shipped her to a California home.

When with much sensitivity I confronted them of why "we" are so reclusive and tight lipped when authorities ask us questions. The response was that we are not withholding any information from them which they can get anyway. If they would have checked the airport documents they would have seen that she had a plane ticket to California.

In other areas I have talked to the police or sheriff departments and they will admit that they experienced that too, about how reclusive the cult is. Shady people must hide from their activities

177

and shady activities. Watch their actions for a while and compare it to the life of Christ and his disciples. They taught openly in the temples and in the country. Even John the Baptist spoke openly of his conviction and belief which resulted in his decapitation and death. The cult hides their beliefs from strangers and they alter their practices when in public. "Hide the sticks, do not kiss greet each other when in public," along with other alterations. Onlookers will not get a complete picture of this cult until they join it, and then only with some time. For that reason I wrote this book to provide the knowledge of error to other people. That way they have a chance that I never had. My family was destroyed by them but I wish this exposure will help others from becoming a victim like I became. The loss of my children from me is almost permanent. Within a few months of no judicial change, I will have lost them forever. I hope you can learn from my mistakes.

CHAPTER 11

ENTERTAINMENT OF RESISTANCE WITH THE CHILDREN

I have my children one time a month. I strive hard at finding activities where I can enjoy my children. Because of the many restrictions within this cult I struggle to create acceptable things to do. The following will give you some ideas of what I am dealing with.

Sinfulness of Carousels

I have taken my children several times to the Milwaukee County Zoo. One time while I was with only my five children, we went to the zoo that had very few people that day and we were able to roam easily. The zoo had a small train ride that goes around the circumference of the grounds. We had enjoyed that ride before in times past. As we approached it this time I noticed the carousel practically empty. I knew the cult in recent years had preached against rides and amusement parks. Never the less, I asked if anybody wanted to go on the Merry-Go-Round which is permissible. The youngest four shouted, "yes" with glee!

I did not notice it but as we went, Rachel, my oldest daughter, was warning the others about the sin of this wicked thing, before we walked the hundred yards. Upon arrival none of the children wanted to go on it anymore. The attitude change was that it was not a Merry-Go-Round, but a sinful carousel and condemning people to hell. There was fear in not obeying the cult's teaching.

While we were at the zoo we went in the gift shop. Now, I do remember that the cult had preached against the game Monopoly. There in the gift shop I see Animalopy, a revised version of Animals in the various spaces instead of Boardwalk and Park Place, and such.

"Hey children, would anybody play this with me in the Motel Room if I bought it?"

They studied the box and saw the "demonic" dice pictured and the answer was, "NO!" Dice are a sin.

Mall of America - "Sinful Attraction"

I was enjoying all of my children one time in Minneapolis and St. Paul. I discreetly pulled Randy and David aside and told them that I wanted to stop at the Mall of America. I told them that I also wanted to take the children on rides in the Mall's center, the Camp Snoopy Amusement Park. We discussed the opposition we would get from Rachel, my oldest daughter, who would know that rides like that are a sin to the Cult. So we agreed upon a plan that might work.

Once in the van the preplanned discussion began. Randy pipes up, "Hey Dad, can we split up in two groups and run around the mall in different areas?"

I played my part. "Well, yeah, I guess so," I said.

"Can I go with Randy?" several of the children ask.

"Wait a minute. I think the four oldest children could take care of themselves. However, I think the three youngest should stay with me," I stated.

They all agreed.

As soon as they were out of sight I took the younger children straight to the center of the building where Camp Snoopy is. I bought tickets for at least two rides each. The Red Barron was a delight to them. "Now which ride do you want to go on?" I asked.

As we walked around, deciding which one, they spotted a carousel. Oops! Suddenly it dawned on them that this must be one of those hell bound places that their Mother's church preaches against. Suddenly the desire for any more rides vanished. They started looking over their shoulder to see if Rachel was coming. To use up the tickets I could only talk them into going on the Red Barron again. I had a few points remaining. I had my sister along for that day and remember having her watch the youngest two while I took Stevie despite his fears of getting caught, to introduce him into something new.

Stevie is my child that was beat by my wife about 300-500 swats in trying to break his stubborn will. He was not submissive when she had ordered him to willfully lay across his bed to receive his punishment. The result was a massive black and blue bruise beating before he could submit. This incident I already mentioned earlier.

Stevie and I climbed the stairs to the roller coaster. How he squealed in extreme delight I will never forget. Seeing his joy made my violation of the cult's rules worth it to me. I wish I could do it again when the children don't have to fear punishment when they get home.

Video Games – Technology of the Devil

I have to be careful here with giving too much detailed information now for the sake of protecting my younger children. This exhibit will wind up in the hands of the cult and I must protect my children from the punishment and rebuke that they would get if I revealed details.

Video games are a sin because there is motion on the screen. However, watching a child hysterically laugh at watching a funny video game is exciting. It is difficult to remain somber while a child verbalizes such great delight when they watch someone run the cars in the video, over fire hydrants and drive through people's yards intentionally. Breaking normal driving practices was hilarious to the children.

Bonduel, Wisconsin- Harley Shop – Sinful and Evil

My ex-wife is constantly moving in pursuit of the cult. If the cult moves, she moves. In the first part of 2007, my children lived with her near Bonduel, Wisconsin, north but mostly west of Green Bay, WI. Alongside of this freeway is a Harley Davidson dealer, not very far from where they lived.

One time, on my way to pick up my children, I stopped there to take a look around. It also was a museum and a small zoo. On the front of the building mounted on the roof, were two cars as if air borne going over the roof of the building. The first was a Dukes of Hazards car being chased by a second car, a black and white police car. Inside was a room filled with rare collector cars and several antique items.

They also had a display of reptiles, alligators, turtles, iguanas, and snakes. One man wrestled with a 4-5 foot gator. I thought it would be interesting to my children if I could get them past the motorcycle and supplies room. I do know the teachings of the cult that motorcycles in general are frowned upon and Harley's are evil and unacceptable.

I remember one time when two church/cult members drove to the Ohio camp meeting on motorcycles. The bikes were quietly banned off the church grounds, and forced to be parked on the neighbor's property. Those two bikes were not even Harleys.

After I picked up my children for the beginning of my placement, I brought them back to this dealership. They didn't want to leave the safety of my vehicle very easily. With much persuasion, they finally came inside and seemed to enjoy seeing the reptiles and touching the large turtles. However, they seemed scared as if God was going to strike them dead if they delayed there much longer.

Water Sports – if wet, then potentially wicked!

It was just basic knowledge within the cult that swimming almost entirely is wrong. Never will a cult family allow even their children to use a swimming pool. Renting a motel room that has a pool or water park is spiritually deplorable and not an option of activity that I can do with my children.

There are four specific sins at risk here; exposure, age, cross gender and undress according to them. This church/cult refers to themselves as the "Saints" and everyone else are the "Aints". A saint does not place themselves at a visual exposure risk with wet clothing except for one time. That only time is when they get "submerged" baptized. When a child reaches puberty, swimming gets eliminated which becomes a age barrier or restriction. Cross gender restrictions are also magnified everywhere. At their camp meetings there are children swings, slides, monkey bars and such. Either only the young boys play on the recreation equipment or just the young girls would play, never both at the same time.

Therefore, that same gender segregation applies in swimming too. Isolated and secluded swim spots are required and then with only my children and then also if they are not mature yet. The last absolute "risk" requirement is the "undress" part. There is a dress code that is absolute 24/7. The clothing is to the ankle with long sleeves buttoned at the neck is mandatory, full time for every activity. Male and female alike, only the hands and face ever gets exposed when other people are around. That includes shaving in the men's bathroom at the camp meetings. It is forbidden for the man to take his shirt off to shave when other men are also using the facility. With that dress code they go to church, but also it is required for every activity including swimming. Swimming in long pants for boys is still easier that what my daughters must abide by. They have never experienced swimming without their ankle length dress on. They don't swim, if it is a problem swimming inside a "sleeping bag" or "parachute". The same church rules are applied for every activity, boating, tubing, canoeing, kayaking, or even things other than water sports like horseback riding or skiing. The young women are usually restricted from that type of 'men' sports.

Wisconsin Dells – mostly a den for devils and demons

There is an extreme limitation at what I can do with my children at the Dells. I have taken them on the army ducks and boat cruises. One time someone gave me free tickets to the Tommy Bartlet Show. According to the cults standards I corrupted my children extensively that day. All shows are shunned. The water slides, roller coasters, go-karts, reverse bungee jumps which sling shoots you up into the air, and other rides were condemned as a sin, but interesting to watch.

There was one very hot day that I remember well. This happened about five years ago. I had all my children that day driving and walking around trying to find something permissible to do which was difficult. In the heat ("90' +) my five year old, the youngest child Bethany, suddenly starts crying and acting strange. Looking back now I realize that she was having a heat exhaustion attack.

We all went to my van and started to think along those lines of what is going on. I then realized how hot she was and I started wetting her down with water. Upon that episode of cooling her down I discovered that the "modesty" of dress was the cause of this life threatening situation. She had on a tee shirt, a full length slip over that, with a full dark color dress with long sleeves and length down to the ankle with, I believe, a vest on top of that. All of my five children must wear something like that even if the temperature is over 90 degrees. Are the church rules on modesty in the "Best Interest of the Children"?

Christmas Shopping – search for the needle in the haystack!

First of all, the cult honors NO holidays. They are Anti-Christmas, Easter, Labor Day, Memorial Day, Independence Day and even Thanksgiving is condemned. "Worship the Turkey" is what I had heard preached. So instead of going Christmas shopping, I go winter gift shopping with my family.

Here is a list of sinful toys. I think at least 95% of toys are considered sinful. All Barbie dolls and celebrity dolls are evil. All other dolls must be capable of being "sanctified", which means the doll has to be dressed the way the cult dresses. If the doll is a child there is more tolerance then if it was a woman doll. A doll of a woman must have long hair so that is can be put up in a bun on the back of her head. The clothing has to be what they call Godly.

Any toys to do with sports cars, racing, race tracks, collector cars, war equipment, vanity vehicles, lively Colored toy vehicles or other toys are all wrong. Most books are usually wrong especially fiction or fables. Coloring books usually are corrupted with "un-sanctified" pictures. Even if a toy is permissible, if the color is "loud", the toy becomes sinful and condemned.

My 5th child Steve, or 6th child Joel was deciding on a bicycle. It looked nice to me. The price range of $50 for each child qualified the bike acceptable in that area also. Then Rachel came over to evaluate it, if it was "saintly" enough for the church standard or if it would get pitched when he brought it home. She whispered something to him and suddenly he didn't want the bike anymore. It was blue but it had orange pin-striping and highlights which were ungodly. There was no "modest" bike in that price range.

I would have bought that bike and kept it at my place if I had a different placement situation. My son would hardly ever be able to ride it under this present condition. In the last couple of years when I was still married and in the mutation of the cult, I had noticed my wife had thrown several brand new toys away which were given to my children from relatives. The relatives did not know that the toys they selected were sinful. I wish you could fathom how extensive this reality really is.

Milwaukee County Museum/simulators-virtual reality to hell!

Shame on me! I knew the cult would disapprove the simulators but my children didn't have the capacity to reason that a simulator is a combination of a movie screen and a carnival "carn-evil" ride. So I stretched their imagination with two "rides".

The children enjoyed going inside this capsule. The door shut and we were off flying a military jet bucking and tilting in our seats to do those acrobatic maneuver. There was a lot of laughter behind those closed doors. I paid for a second ride with them not knowing what I got. This time they "kind of" experienced what a roller coaster is like for the very first time ever, except for Stevie who had at Camp Snoopy experienced a real one. It was sure a delight to experience the laughter and screaming inside that capsule. It was hard to believe that we stayed in that spot the entire time.

Randy, David, (my two oldest) and I have spent a day alone in Wisconsin Dells when I received two free tickets once for one of those parks. They enjoyed roller coasters and slides.

The next time we went to the museum, the five children all refused to partake of the simulator. The cult must have educated them about the wickedness and destination of hell if they participated in watching a "devil vision" (television) while their seat is being tipped every which way. It is nothing else!

Chicago Museum of Science and Industry – why those wicked screens

I thought the place was very impressive! However, I could not experience everything about it and how the submarine was captured. That is because a lot of the information was revealed on movie screen. We as a family leave one room and go into the next. It appears that you are standing on the deck of a ship with water all around. The real wall is actually a movie screen from floor to ceiling. On the screen you see a ship or the submarine in the ocean. There is ocean all around you. There is a captivating voice recorded that has a play by play scenario of what is taking place.

I wish I could have stayed there and witnessed the "capture" or whatever it was. However, my children saw that it was a movie screen and quickly moved on to the next room. It was busy that day with a lot of people, so for the safety of my children, I had to move on.

As a person leaves from one of the rooms, you enter a large area that has the submarine on display. You enter the room higher up and walk down a long ramp parallel with the submarine. Near the bottom is a photographer who stops each person, couple or group and takes a picture. The person gets a code number and later gets the opportunity to buy the picture. I am glad that I bought ours.

Control by Fear

Why would my children want to live with such fanatical rules? Is it not true that my children upon questioning them, would respond that they don't like movie screens, rides, or the rest that I mentioned here? That is true, but WHY? Until a person experiences what I have experienced, they will not comprehend what fear there is by the members of this group. By that FEAR they have control.

I wish everyone could go to my website, www.screwedkenoshastyle.com, click on the "church that took my family", find the audio section, and then listen to the five minute portion of the Susan Mutch Sermon. That screaming is common to that church for their style of preaching. Screaming, "hell, torment, gnashing of teeth, lost, fire, doomed for eternity!" for two hours to a young child creates fear. However, that is still only in generality, because it is screamed out at the entire group. What if however, it was only yelled at you? What if you are the only one in the room besides one or more of the pastors doing the yelling in your face? Now it becomes personal and internally tormenting. That is when your FEAR becomes gruesomely haunting inside of you.

I have witnessed numerous people get that treatment before it was my turn. I saw the victims come out of that "room" terrified, in many parts of this country and Canada while at meetings. Each time though, they were (all victims) obviously shook up and crying or with blood shot eyes from crying. I have witnessed the harsh treatment of excommunication and shunning that this group does. I feel sorry for the children that still live within the cult family like my children are. They are too young to escape. The shunning torment is so great and over powering that almost all a child can do is run to the altar, crying and begging for forgiveness. The conditions for forgiveness is to submit to this torment of fear by following the rules and teachings of the ministry. That is considered righteous Godly fear.

I know what that torment of fear is all about, I experienced it first-hand. The pastor ordered my family to not leave Kenosha to visit my Dad and siblings in Minnesota. I violated his orders in 2001 and also in 2002. That is the reason why I am in court and have experienced jail. The pastor told my wife to leave me and she did.

June 2008

Because of the Kenosha court system favoring Shereen, I have fought for six years without getting justice. The sequel to this book, "Fighting the Black Robe Conspiracy", which I intend to write immediately after this book, I will elaborate on why I went to jail and the details of how I came to that trauma with details and my experiences. I have had five judges so far that have recused themselves off my case already. If there were not mistakes made which they don't want to correct, why would they remove themselves from my case?

I paid for a hearing to get the mistakes corrected. The judges rescheduled my hearings several times before the fifth judge just simply threw me in jail. That happened on November 16, 2007, without getting the unbiased hearing I paid for. So I was in jail separated from my children for six months. My very first chance of seeing them since October 2007, was now in June of 2008. The following troubles are because the cult had about eight months to program my children to condemn, shun, and train them how to be malicious and defiant toward me.

I call Shereen up on Wednesday, to notify her that I cannot pick up the children on the scheduled time by the court. I will be late more than a full day for my full week placement. I will pick them up on Sunday afternoon. Oh, what a fight!

"Yes, technically you have the children this week, but you didn't give me enough notice of your plans", she insists.

"What do you mean?", I object. "You knew it since September of last year when it was established in the courts that this was my week. Why, isn't nine months enough notice?"

There was a lot more arguments of why the children cannot come with me. They have a wedding in the church the Saturday that I have them, and the children really wanted to go to that. They will give me problems if I don't cancel my time with them for they have plans. I have plans too!

"I will come down to Ohio, and if I don't get the children, I will only drive back to Kenosha so that I can file contempt papers against you on Monday morning." I finished up with and hung up.

True and accurate, they did give me problems! There was nothing that I could do right. My oldest daughter, Rachel, was more than a challenge. She would try to intentionally pick a fight. I was shocked at her disrespect of looking me in the face, and then with all her cult-ish venom and fury, spew out her disgust at me. With no less malicious fervor than the pastor that yelled in my face, she squinted her eyes with hatred, and dumped her animosity upon me.

"You are disgusting!", she glares at me. "You need to get saved because you are fighting against God's true church. You are touching the apple of God's eye. I don't want to see you ever again, or until you get saved.", she fiercely spews out in disdain. Unless you can picture a violent look with an extreme harsh tone, you don't have the picture of how it was said.

It appeared that the children intentionally tried to trash everything they could. Their response was that, "If you want us, then you have to take care of us!" After they left I needed to clean my car. That is when I noticed that they had created about a five inch thick mess on the floor in the back seat. They had wrappings, paper cups and plates, and other garbage soaked into one massive disgusting mess. They must have poured a gallon of water on it to get it that soggy. That was just one of the many messes.

They had a cellphone which they used probably daily. Was it coincidence or am I paranoid? It seemed that right after that they had called home, that within minutes more arguments started. It seemed that a new spurt of malicious energy was released immediately after they hung up. The quarreling onslaught that they gave me became so overwhelming that I was forced to take them to the children's / Social Services in Minnesota. That helped a little but the cult coaching them still continued by cellphone.

They made an intentional mess for my other friends and relatives so that they commented about what corrupt children they were. Some of my relatives made the comment that Rachel the oldest is not really welcome to their house anymore. She was so rude and controlling the other children to do wrong. Bethany, my youngest child spilled lemonade on the carpet. She was ready to clean up her mess when Rachel motioned for her to not do it. My sister caught that gesture with Bethany's quick change of direction even though Rachel denies that she ordered it.

I am sorry about the last few paragraphs sounding like I am just whining about little stuff. However, without sharing the little situations of what is taking place, it is impossible to portray the attitudes or spirit of this battle. A very hostile war was going on. The cult was using my children as the artillery in attempts to destroy me. It is nearly impossible to explain to an outsider the shunning and alienation that takes place beyond the visual level.

July 2008

I drove the nearly eight hundred miles one way to get my children for that month's placements. Half way there I call them to notify that I am already on my way. Shereen puts the children on the phone to argue with me. They tell me to turn around and go back home, that they don't want to go with me. How can I grasp someone out of the jaws of the cult when they don't even consider themselves in danger?

I tell them that I will be there in the morning and tell them "good bye", and hang up. They accuse me then of hanging up on them. They just wanted to argue on the phone to use up my minutes. I knew that there was going to be problems the next morning.

So the next morning I went straight to the Greenville, Ohio sheriff station. After listening to what I had to say, they accepted my request for an escort. Things were not any better at the house when we arrived there. Shereen glared at me when she answered the door and without saying a word she went back in. Then all five children came out and argued that they don't want to go with me. They made up stories that they are afraid of me and don't trust me. Without understanding the underlying spirit behind all of this, it would seem best if the children did not come with me. The fear can have a deeper meaning.

Yes, it is a fear that I might corrupt them with normal activities of common people, but which is condemned by the cult. I am too crafty at bringing subtle "sin" into their life, like I mentioned in the Milwaukee simulator section. If they spent time with me, they might start to doubt the authenticity of the cult. They might start to question some of their teachings. Therefore I am a great threat to them.

After much arguing I realized that they will not come with me no matter how long I tried to persuade them. I tried giving them a hug and was rejected each time until I got to Joel. He allowed me to give him a hug which let me then hug the others also. I left in tears wishing them the best.

As I left with tears streaming down my face, my mind raced through the many years of memories. I loved my children and thought about the many delightful things we had done together. I thought of cute things that each child had done and what they meant to me. It was not them that just rejected me, but the cult had twisted their minds to say those things. As I write this book I know my small space of opportunity is closing fast and actually almost shut already. At best I only have a few months and they will be gone forever. Follow the money trail and a person can see why the courts have deprived my children from me so far. I wish I could sell twenty or thirty thousand copies of this book this year to pay for the best attorney. If I don't, I will lose my children to the cult probably forever. Why can "justice" be bought? And what will happen to those authorities that accepted this blood money?

CHAPTER 12

<u>"WHEN WILL YOU EVER</u>
<u>QUIT HATING THE CULT?"</u>

There have been a few people that have asked me something like that along those lines. I need to modify or correct that misconception. First of all, I must mention that I heard a wide range of comments made by other individuals that I told some of my experiences to, which I wrote about in this book. They were typically hostile in nature. Some mentioned that I must be a stronger person than they are. If the pastor had poked his finger in their face and screaming all that nonsense, the pastor would have gotten his finger or face rearranged differently. There were many violent comments from inflicting pain all the way to killing the pastor, the wife, or any other member involved.

I am sorry for getting misinterpreted that I want to do the same. Yes, I do despise what they have done to me, and wish that the common law of justice could equalize out the malicious wrongs that were done. I am not so pure and perfect that I would desire nothing to happen to these liars and cruel instigators. I do long for recompense to be done to them. However, I do not have any murderous hatred against any of them personally. Often I fantasize over getting presented with an opportunity of either my ex-wife, any cult pastor, or any of the Judges or attorneys, to be stranded with a life threatening situation. Without hesitation I would love to jump right into the situation to save their life.

One example is, suppose I was driving down a road that is deserted with only one vehicle in front of me. Suddenly as if the driver in front of me fell asleep, he veers across both lanes and plummets down into a river below. Suppose that he did not die on impact but was unable to free himself to escape the inevitable death without help. I leave my car and run down to the river and then suddenly realize that the driver is either, Danny Layne, Pat

O'Shea, or any of my other "enemies". Am I crazy to wish for such an opportunity to show them what Jesus would do? Without hesitation, I would jump right in to rescue them to the best of my capacity. No, I don't HATE anyone.

My greatest regret with this excommunication, shunning, and divorce is all the friends that I lost. There are a lot of very nice people in that cult. I sure wish that I could see them and talk to them. But that is nothing but a pipe dream or illusion, since they are forced to shun me for their own safety. I also regret not seeing some of my former in-laws. There were a lot of nice relatives of Shereen's that I long to see, but that too was destroyed by the divorce.

The absolute worst is the separation from my children. My greatest goal for writing this book is to warn others, and to make enough money from it to be able to hire the best attorney to straighten this mess out. I want to thank you for reading this book. If any of this information stirred you and you wish you could help, please spread this book to your friends, co-workers, your church members, or whoever you get in contact with. I need help and I need it fast. Without your help my battle of desire is lost. I can make it until I die, but many other people besides my children are at great danger. I don't know who said it first, but there is a quote that I will finish up with now. "THE EASIEST WAY FOR EVIL TO PREVAIL IS FOR GOOD PEOPLE TO DO NOTHING!"

Made in the USA
Monee, IL
29 July 2022